Please renew/return this item by the last date shown.

So that your telephone call is charged at local rate, please call the numbers as set out below:

	From Area codes 01923 or 020:	From the rest of Herts:
Renewals:	01923 471373	01438 737373
Enquiries:	01923 471333	01438 737333
Textphone:	01923 471599	01438 737599

L32   www.hertsdirect.org/librarycatalogue

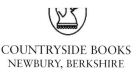

COUNTRYSIDE BOOKS
NEWBURY, BERKSHIRE

COUNTRYSIDE BOOKS
3 Catherine Road
Newbury, Berkshire

To view our complete range of books,
please visit us at
www.countrysidebooks.co.uk

ISBN 978 1 84674 210 1

Designed by Peter Davies, Nautilus Design
Typeset by Mac Style, Beverley, East Yorkshire
Produced through MRM Associates Ltd., Reading
Printed by Information Press, Oxford

Contents

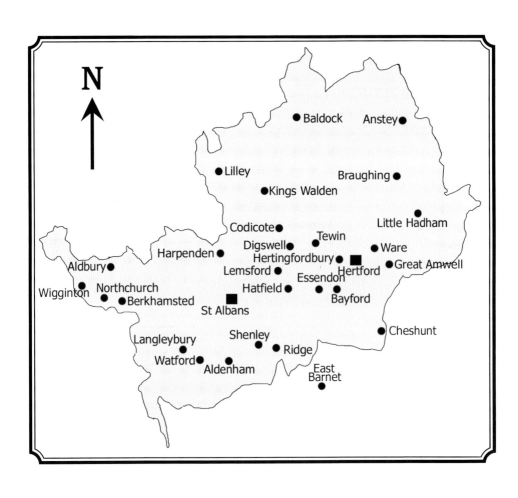

Introduction

I have always had a weakness for wandering in churchyards, and a tendency to stop in front of an old stone and muse, 'I wonder who they were?'. Often it has meant going home with a name and dates scrawled on a scrap of paper and spending time, when I should have been doing other things, in happily tracking them down in books, newspapers and online, sometimes producing whole family trees from one gravestone.

Hertfordshire has some wonderful churchyards to meander around on a sunny day. London may be seeping slowly into our southern parts, but get into the north, east or west of the county and you can be miles from anywhere, with no other human being in sight and only the sounds of birds singing and the wind in the trees. Sometimes, it's true, a village church is not in the most obvious place and you have to search a little for it, but that is part of the pleasure and it is usually well worth the effort.

Memorials can vary from family mausoleums to simple headstones, some with inscriptions so faded as to be almost unreadable. I say 'almost' because one group of people who can decipher anything humanly possible are the members of the Hertfordshire Family History Society. The Society began a project some years ago to record the monumental inscriptions (MIs) in every churchyard in the county, and year by year they produce informative booklets that are invaluable to churchyard wanderers (see their website www.hertsfhs.org.uk for more information). There is nothing like finding things when you least expect them, but it's a great help if there is a map and a record of what is actually on the stone!

The stories in this book can only scratch the surface of the number that can be told and it has been hard deciding who to choose to write about. Some people I would have included, I have already written about in my book *Hertfordshire Heroes*, and they are not to be found repeated here. So instead these 'tales' cover a variety of life and experience. They include the parish clerk of Anstey, as well as an Archbishop of Canterbury; a man who was buried twice and a man who was nearly buried before he was dead; a man who died at Trafalgar with Admiral Lord Nelson, and a man who witnessed the death of Captain James Cook in the South Seas; two war widows and Hertfordshire's first Victoria Cross winner. I have deliberately only chosen memorials that are outside the church as, sadly, these days churches are sometimes kept locked and it would be a shame to have a wasted journey.

Discovering other people's stories is a fascinating pastime, coupled with some beautiful scenery. It can sometimes be amusing, sometimes moving, and I hope you enjoy these stories and that they will inspire you to go out and make your own discoveries in Hertfordshire's churchyards.

Margaret Ward

Acknowledgements

I would like to thank my friends Maureen Jones, Elaine Tyler and Nigel Goose for their help and support – and their photographs; and Peter Buttle for the photograph of the tomb of Nicholas Hawksmoor and permission to use it.

ALDBURY

MRS HUMPHRY WARD – 'ONE OF THE LAST OF THE GREAT VICTORIANS'

When Mrs Humphry Ward died on 24 March 1920, she was described in her obituary in *The Times* as 'one of the last of the great Victorians'. Just over 30 years before, when her novel *Robert Elsmere* was published, no less a figure than Tolstoy had called her 'the greatest of living English novelists', who could number Prime Minister Gladstone and the eminent author Henry James among her fans. Yet it would be hard now to find anyone who knows of her, or has read any of her published novels. She is buried here in Aldbury churchyard, with her husband, Thomas Humphry Ward.

Mary Augusta Arnold was born in 1851 in Tasmania but her family links were firmly English. She was the granddaughter of Dr Arnold, headmaster of Rugby School – made famous in literature by *Tom Brown's Schooldays* – and niece of the poet Matthew Arnold. Her father brought the family back to England in 1856 and they settled in Oxford, where Mary went through a course of self-education by taking advantage of being able to study and read in the Bodleian Library.

While at Oxford, in 1872, she met and married Thomas Humphry Ward, who became tutor of Brasenose College, and, as was the custom of the time, for the rest of her life she was publicly known only by her married name, Mrs Humphry Ward.

She had been writing for her own pleasure for some years by then, but now began getting articles accepted for publication. Between 1881 and 1920 she wrote 31 books, plus many articles, and her income from writing formed the basis of the family finances. In 1919 she was awarded the CBE.

In 1881 her husband Thomas left Oxford to take a post on *The Times* and the family moved to London. In 1892 they rented the Georgian country house called Stocks near Aldbury, later buying it outright. Mary wrote with delight: 'At Stocks I shall be able to see something of the genuine English country life.' Thanks to Mary's writing, they were able to keep the house in fashionable London, as well as this country retreat for the summer and holidays. Stocks meant a lot to Mary, particularly the gardens, and she took happily to being 'lady of the manor'. She and Thomas came regularly to church services, she visited the poor and took them little gifts of coal or vegetables, and organised entertainments for the villagers. In London, too, she worked hard on philanthropic ventures in the East End, particularly involving herself in the founding of the Passmore Edwards Settlement in 1897, later renamed Mary Ward House and an innovative venture providing poor children with play and sports facilities, with a school for physically handicapped children alongside. Selected poor children and families were also brought out of the city to Stocks, to a cottage on the estate, for a breath of country air.

However, life was not so straightforward or as placid as this very Victorian scenario would suggest. Her son Arthur (who was to be elected Liberal Unionist MP for West Herts 1910-1918) ran up huge gambling debts and her husband tended to spend her money almost as soon as she earned it, on pictures and fine antiques. She also suffered increasingly debilitating bad health, not helped by the fact that she simply had to keep working to support the family.

One of the most interesting things about this 'great Victorian' is the paradox of her life and beliefs. Having had to educate herself, for instance, in 1879 she was instrumental in the campaign for and founding of Somerville Hall at Oxford, with twelve young ladies as its first intake. A great supporter of higher education for women, yet she did not make sure her own daughters had the formal education she had yearned for herself.

She was a very powerful, hardworking woman for a cause she believed in, with the ability to persuade and to organise, and 'an excellent woman of business', which makes it even stranger that she vehemently opposed women being given the vote. In what her biographer John Sutherland called 'one of the most

A well placed seat marks the location of Mrs Humphry Ward's headstone.

unequivocally misguided decisions of her career', in 1908 she founded the Women's National Anti-Suffrage League. The opening declaration of the League asserted: 'The association will represent those who believe that, though Mrs Fawcett [leader of the suffrage agitators] is personally well fitted to have a vote, or many votes, that is a poor reason for admitting to the franchise two or three millions of women who know nothing whatever of politics, or parties, or the nation, or the Empire.' Mrs Humphry Ward devoted a great deal of time and her considerable ability to the cause of obstructing a reform we can look back on and see as inevitable, and which now seems a sad waste of her talents.

Mary died at her London house but her funeral was held at Aldbury on 27 March 1920, with the service conducted by the Dean of St Paul's Cathedral, Dean Inge, who eulogised her as 'perhaps the greatest Englishwoman of our time'. Her coffin was carried on a bier from Stocks to the church, borne by some of the gardeners, and with her family following on foot. A ceremonial procession of members of the Hertfordshire Constabulary walked before the coffin – an official courtesy that reflected her appointment as one of the first women magistrates in the country, only the month before. Her husband Thomas died in 1926 and is buried here with her, against the hedge to the right behind the church, while her son Arthur also lies in the churchyard.

ALDENHAM

PLAGUE AND WAR

Thomas Carlyle Parkinson

The simple headstone of Thomas Carlyle Parkinson bears the words: 'born at Sydney NSW 17 February 1884, died in faithful discharge of scientific duties at Aldenham 4 February 1909'. The obvious question is, what 'scientific duties' could have been so dangerous as to cause his death in this peaceful place?

The answer lies in the serum laboratories of the Lister Institute, situated since 1903 at Queensbury Lodge, about two miles from Elstree. The Lister Institute, initially called the British Institute of Preventive Medicine, was founded in 1891 to study the causes, prevention and treatment of infectious diseases in man and animals. Rabies was the main fear at the time, and there was nowhere in England that this deadly disease could be controlled – anyone bitten by a rabid animal faced a long journey to Paris to the Institut Pasteur if they wanted the latest treatments.

The grinding process that was used in the production of the serums for rabies and other contagious diseases was highly dangerous for the men engaged on the work; two researchers at the Lister died of typhoid in the early 1900s. And the Lister was soon involved in work that brought its scientists into contact with one of the most feared of all human diseases – plague, in both its pneumonic and bubonic forms.

At the end of the 19th century a new epidemic of the plague seemed imminent, spreading out around the world from Hong Kong, via India. A seaman brought the disease to the port of London in 1896 and there was a small outbreak in Glasgow in 1900. In 1903, in India, half a million people died of the plague. Scientists and guest workers from all over the world came to the Lister to work at what was the cutting edge of research. One of them was a young Australian, Thomas Carlyle Parkinson.

The work on the plague antitoxin and vaccine was carried out in an isolated laboratory in the grounds of the Institute, and anyone who thought they might have accidentally touched the bacillus would immediately bathe in Lysol. However, familiarity breeds carelessness and at the beginning of February 1909 Parkinson began to feel very ill indeed. At first he thought it was influenza, but when his lungs became infected tests showed that he had contracted pneumonic plague. Three days later he was dead, and the 25-year-old was buried here at Aldenham, far from his home country, probably the last person in Hertfordshire to die of the plague.

The year after his death at least four people died in a limited outbreak of the plague in Suffolk, but by now the link between fleas, rats and humans had been established and the disease could never again hold quite the grip of fear it had done for centuries. The Lister continued in its vital research work. After all, as the headstone on Thomas Carlyle Parkinson's grave reminds us:

'So many worlds, so much to do.'

Midshipman Robert Smith

Nearby, the death of an even younger man is commemorated. The flat ledger stone, lying flush with the grass, of Philip Bellona Smith of Aldenham Place bears also reference to his older brother, Midshipman Robert Smith, who was killed on board the *Victory* at the Battle of Trafalgar, on 21 October 1805.

In 1805 Britain faced invasion by Napoleon, who had built up a flotilla of gun-boats at Boulogne, with over 100,000 men ready to cross the Channel. The great Admiral Lord Nelson on his flagship, the *Victory*, had been lured away from home waters to follow the French and Spanish fleets to the West Indies, but returned in time to engage Napoleon's forces at Trafalgar and win the day. Robert Smith was on that voyage – he had been at sea since 1802 and volunteered for the *Victory* in 1803.

The Smith graves, including that commemorating Midshipman Robert Smith, lie to the right of the path from the side lychgate.

In 1905, on the centenary of the battle, the Aldenham parish magazine printed Robert's last letter home, by courtesy of his nephew, written on the eve of battle. In it you can hear the echoes of so many letters written by sailors and soldiers in such circumstances over the centuries. Knowing that his parents would only read it if he was killed, 20-year-old Robert wanted particularly that they should 'not give way to any uneasiness on my account and further that you my dearest of Mothers will not give way to those low spirits which you are subject to, consider that your affectionate son could not die in a more glorious cause and that it is all the fortune of war.'

The next day he died fighting alongside his hero, Lord Horatio Nelson, when, in the dreadful carnage of close contact cannon fire, his legs were shot off and he bled to death. In 2005, on the bicentenary of Trafalgar, the church bells at Aldenham rang out in his memory.

Lt Colonel Dalrymple

If you wander around the churchyard, you can't help but be surprised by the number of old (and not so old) warriors who lie here. Even the gravestones have had their brush with war: the pockmarks on those to the south of the church are not due to weathering or vandalism, but to a close encounter with German bombs in the Second World War, on 16 October 1940.

To the east of the church, for instance, is the altar tomb of the Dalrymple family, who lived at Delrow House. It records the death of Leighton Cathcart Dalrymple: Companion of the Order of the Bath and Lieutenant Colonel of the 15th King's Hussars, 'at the head of which gallant regiment he highly distinguished himself at the Battle of Waterloo, where he had three horses kill'd under him and after receiving two contusions towards the close of the memorable day his left leg was carried off by a cannonball.'

He survived the wound and came home to Delrow House, only to die in 1820 at the age of 35, 'deeply deplored by his parents'.

The pockmarks left by shrapnel from a Second World War bomb.

Perhaps he felt satisfied that he had restored the family honour. His father, General Sir Hew Dalrymple, had been at one time commanding officer in the Peninsular Wars but was recalled to England, his limitations laughingly captured by his nickname – 'Dowager Dalrymple'. His subordinate, Arthur Wellesley, went on to become Duke of Wellington and to defeat Napoleon at Waterloo, in the process becoming one of the greatest heroes of the age.

ANSTEY

THOMAS BARKER – PARISH CLERK

Thomas Barker was 'admitted as Church Clerk' in 1834, as his gravestone at the side of the church path, near the double gates, tells us, and went on to fill the post for the next 60 years.

The parish clerk was a layman who acted as the priest's right-hand man. This was an important job in the community and originally the post might have been filled by a person who would otherwise have aspired to become a clergyman, but perhaps was prevented because of poverty. Parish clerks often saw themselves as very important people, second to none in the parish hierarchy – there was even a Livery Company of the City of London for parish clerks! They got a small payment, which varied from parish to parish, but could charge fees for each and everything a parishioner might need at some time in their lives, such as tolling the bell for a funeral, churching a woman after birth, etc. They might also write up the parish register entries of baptisms, marriages and funerals, though strictly speaking this was illegal.

Thomas Barker's gravestone leans towards the church path.

In some places the clerk was appointed by the vicar, in others it was the parishioners who chose him by election. It was a rule that he had to be at least 20 years old, and an original church requirement was that he be competent in reading, writing and singing. On appointment the clerk was licensed by the bishop, and had to take an oath to obey the incumbent.

In the days before organ music became common in churches, the music often had to be played on their own instruments by a group of parishioners, or else hymn-singing had to be unaccompanied. Up to the early 19th century the parish clerk's musical ability was very important. At Shenley in the south of the county an epitaph for Joseph Rogers, parish clerk from 1791, reads:

Silent in dust lies mould'ring here
A Parish Clerk with voice most clear
None Joseph Rogers could excel
In laying bricks and singing well.

We don't know about Thomas Barker's vocal abilities, but a description of him was included in *Anstey: A Hertfordshire Parish*, by Frank Ricardo Williams in 1929: 'Thomas Barker was a remarkable man and lived before the time of village schools. He went to work at a very early age, taking care of the sheep by the side of the road. He determined, however, that he would obtain some education, and in his spare intervals studied a reading book, and when he met with difficulties he could not solve, it was his custom to stop and ask the help of the first passer-by whom he saw.

'During the time he was church clerk, till old age came upon him, he made notes in a book of all marriages, baptisms and funerals.

'He generally entered the names of the churchwardens, overseers and surveyors: occasionally he mentioned Easter vestry meetings. He kept a very careful account of all fees and gifts he received as church clerk: here and there he gave details of personal expenditure, and matters of interest in connection with the church. Occasionally secular matters are also mentioned, as how to make ginger beer, and how to cure rheumatism, and a charm against ague is given, and certain quarterly passwords of some society he was interested in.'

In 1844 an Act transferred most of the parish clerk's duties to the curate – e.g. helping with services and 50 years later, in 1894, another Act removed most of his other duties, in effect reducing them to the care of documents and maps etc (which would now go to the clerk of the parish council).

When Thomas died in January 1895, his daughter Mrs Emma Wick succeeded him as parish clerk of Anstey and herself was a 'pillar of the church'. There was nothing to stop a woman holding such a post, though it was unusual. Together, she and her father held office for almost 90 years.

As you leave by the lychgate, don't miss the Parish Cage – one of the bays of the gate was bricked in and an iron-studded door put on the church side, with iron bars at the top for ventilation. It would be used as a 'lock-up' for any villager who got into trouble, quite often for being drunk and disorderly! Mrs Wick told Frank Williams the story of an old man on his deathbed – 'Will you bury me outside the Cage? Many a time have I been shut inside and now I want to be outside.' Apparently, his wish was granted. It was in use up to the First World War, but in later years the church coal was kept in there.

The unusual lychgate had one side made into a secure village lock-up, or cage.

BALDOCK

MASTER OF COMEDIANS AND MASTER BREWER

Nathaniel Herbert

On a gravestone behind the church of St Mary the Virgin, by the path, there is a worn carving – could this be a representation of a jester, with cap and bells? If it is, this may be the grave of Nathaniel Herbert, who died on 16 September 1787 and was described in the *Gentleman's Magazine* as 'formerly master of a company of comedians'. When he died, Herbert was the innkeeper at the White Hart in Hitchin Street. He wouldn't have been the first, or the last, man to retire from the stage and take up the life of a publican.

The definition of 'comedian' has changed slightly over time. In Herbert's day, it meant someone who performed on the stage outside London – any provincial actor was by definition a comedian. The life of a strolling player had always been a hard one, on the edge of society and quite often in trouble with the authorities.

After the Restoration of the Monarchy in 1660 the only theatres in England that were allowed to stage drama were at Covent Garden and Drury Lane in London, and to put on a play anywhere else was illegal, such was the fear of subversive elements spreading unrest. This situation gradually changed over time as one by one, provincial venues were given licences as 'royal' theatres, but there was a very clear line drawn (in official eyes, anyway) between the dramatic

A jester and a comedian's cap adorn two headstones in Baldock churchyard.

actor and the strolling player – who got round the ban by putting on plays, but 'disguising' them with musical interludes or comedy routines. Local magistrates would usually turn a blind eye if the master of the company asked nicely enough beforehand for permission to stage a performance.

In 1737 the Licensing Act was passed in an attempt at a bit of a crackdown. Anyone performing at a venue – be it a theatre, a room in an inn, a barn or a field – without a licence from the Lord Chamberlain was 'deemed to be a Rogue and a Vagabond', which meant the full weight of the law could be brought to bear to get them to move on. This was the climate in which Nathaniel Herbert would have taken his company of comedians on tour and it seems highly likely that one of his stopping places was here at Baldock: there was once a theatre in Pond Lane which was later converted into an Independent Chapel. Most such companies developed a regular circuit, so that they would be expected in a place at certain times each year, and their travelling was usually done in the summer months, moving out from their winter home when the roads had dried up enough to be passable.

As master of the company, Herbert would have been responsible for getting bookings, approaching local JPs or mayors for permission to stay, finding performers and getting them and all their paraphernalia from place to place. Theatrical performances in the 18th century were rowdy, casual and boisterous, and that was only the audience! Many companies divided up the takings between them, with some adjustment for seniority. Herbert must have done well out of his time on the road to be able to take on the White Hart in a bustling town like Baldock.

James Ind

Brewing and malting have always been of the utmost importance to this town's prosperity and one of the notable local families of the 18th and early 19th centuries was that of the Inds. James Ind lies here, 'of the Parish, Brewer', who died on 28 November 1810 aged 57, with his wife Mary, and nearby their son James who survived his father by less than a year and died in June 1811, aged just 23.

The Ind family came originally from Cambridge but by the late 1700s James senior owned a brewery and 20 tied houses in and around Baldock, as well as land in four counties. The Ind Brewery in Baldock was on the corner of White

Horse Street and Clothall Road, but the original buildings were demolished not long after his death and replaced by the maltings of James Pryor. The Ind family lived in the large and imposing residence that today is the Zeus Hotel and Restaurant in the High Street.

The eldest son of the family, Edward, purchased the Star Inn and Brewery at Romford in Essex in 1799 and built it up into a highly successful business. In 1845 C.E. Coope joined the firm and in 1886 the familiar Ind Coope label was born.

And ...

Before leaving, wander towards the side of the churchyard that extends down Church Street to discover by the path the grave of little Henry George Brown, who died in 1861, aged 10 years and 10 months:

> *How soon I was cut down, when innocent at play,*
> *The wind it blew a scaffold down and took my life away.*

Then if you take the path back towards the gate onto Hitchin Street, scramble up the grassy bank on the left to give a gentle knock on the side of the large white chest tomb – Clarkson is the name upon it – enclosed by iron railings. No, no one will knock back, it just comes as a surprise to hear the hollow ring. This is not stone but cast iron, made by the Brown Iron Foundry of Clerkenwell in 1830. Here is buried William Clarkson, who as the inscription says, 'zealously supported his friend Thomas Clarkson' in the fight to end slavery in the early 1800s (see Watford).

BAYFORD

WILLIAM YARRELL – NATURALIST

You cannot miss the Yarrell family burial plot at Bayford – it forms what is almost a mini-graveyard within the churchyard, surrounded by iron railings. The most famous member of the family was the naturalist William Yarrell, whose *History of British Fishes* and *History of British Birds* became highly popular standard

The Yarrell family plot, surrounded by iron railings.

works when they were published in the 1830s and 1840s. Several bird species were named after him, including the British pied wagtail – *Motacilla alba yarrellii*.

Born in 1784, by trade William was a bookseller in St James's, Piccadilly, where he took over his father's business. He never married and was described as a man of 'retiring manners and extremely punctual habits', but for all that he was good company and a great diner-out who 'sang a capital song'. Ironically, his early interest in wildlife went no further than to kill it; in those days it did not seem strange to be both a sportsman and a naturalist. He was renowned as an angler and a great marksman as a young man – 'he could bring down a dozen brace of sparrows, from the trap, with his double-barrelled Manton [shotgun], running ...'.

Then, in middle age, he gave up shooting at birds and began to study them. His first published work was *On the Occurrence of Some Rare British Birds*, written for the Royal Institution in 1825, and from that point he became an active member of the naturalist community. He was one of the first members of the new Zoological Society of London and helped to found the Royal Entomological

Society of London. He was elected a Fellow of the Linnaean Society, but his attempt in the 1820s to become a Fellow of the Royal Society failed – his bookselling 'trade' background meant that not even his scientific credentials could gain him sufficient support to be elected.

What made William's work so popular with the book-buying public was his ability to write clearly and simply, yet with accuracy and authority. His books were also well illustrated, and his admiration for the engraver Thomas Bewick was demonstrated by his naming of the Bewick Swan in 1830, shortly after Bewick's death in 1828 – William was the first to realise that this was a distinct species.

William died at the age of 72 in 1856 when he was on a visit to Great Yarmouth (of 'ossification of the heart', according to *The Times*) and his body was brought to Bayford, where his mother's family farmed at Claypits Farm, to be buried with his parents and siblings. The inscription on his headstone reads: 'He was the survivor of twelve brothers and sisters, who, with their father and mother, are all placed close to this spot. First and last, the earliest summon'd and the longest spared are here deposited'.

His admirers also raised a memorial to him at St James' church, Piccadilly, where the executors of his will put up a wall plaque, with swans prominent in its decoration!

BERKHAMSTED

LOVE AND THE HANGMAN

Mary Page

Mary Page, who died in 1865, aged 75, must have been a girl with good looks and plenty of charm as well as intelligence, as she captivated a French king, entertained a queen and ran a successful business in the heart of Berkhamsted.

She lies in Three Close Lane cemetery, which was opened in 1842 when the churchyard at St Peter's could take no more burials. It lies off the High Street, up Rectory Lane, and is a quiet sanctuary from the busy main road.

Mary was one of three daughters of John Page, who was master of the King's Arms in the High Street. This was no ordinary inn. It was a busy coaching stop on a major stagecoach route, known to have stabling for over 40 horses, and ran its own coaches to London. In the 18th and 19th centuries, inns such as this were often the principal meeting places of a town and the King's Arms had assembly rooms for balls and concerts, as well as plenty of room to house civic dinners and society meetings, coroner's courts and the local petty and licensing sessions, so that it functioned as a courtroom also. John Page was the High Constable for the locality, and the local postmaster too, a sensible arrangement when the mail coaches stopped at his inn.

Mary (or Polly as she is sometimes called), Sarah and Catherine helped their father in the running of the inn and Mary was said to have had an 'eye for the aristocracy'. She really struck gold when she caught the attention of Louis XVIII of

The head and foot stones that mark Mary Page's resting place in Three Close Lane cemetery.

France, who used to come regularly to the King's Arms to further his acquaintance with her. From 1807 to 1814 Louis was living in exile in Aylesbury, having left France hurriedly during the French Revolution and the rise of Napoleon Bonaparte. He was the younger brother of Louis XVI, who had died on the guillotine, and was about 50 years of age when pretty Polly, then aged about 17, captivated him.

In 1814 he went back to France after the fall of Bonaparte, but proved so reactionary as king that there was a rise in popular feeling against him. Bonaparte rode that swell to return from his own exile on Elba and Louis had to flee France once more, this time to Ghent, until after the Battle of Waterloo in 1815. Louis died in 1824, but when he was back on the throne of France he kept a promise to Mary and invited her to Versailles, where she apparently had a thoroughly good time. What did Berkhamsted and the King's Arms look like to her when she returned after that glimpse of vast riches?

Her next recorded brush with royalty was in 1841. Her father had by this time died, aged 92, and Mary was in charge at the inn. Queen Victoria, then only four years on the throne and still a pretty young thing, stopped here at the King's Arms to change horses. Great preparations were made for refreshments and entertainment, but the visit was marred for the girls when Mary's sister, Sarah, died suddenly.

There is still a reminder of that royal visit to Berkhamsted in the apple world, as a local gardener named a new apple after the Prince Regent. It became known as 'Lane's Prince Albert'.

Mary and Catherine continued to run the King's Arms until the 1850s and by 1861 they had retired together to a house on Berkhamsted Common. Mary died in 1865, and Catherine (or Katharine, as she now seems to have spelled her name) moved to Castle Street, where she lived alone until her death. It is amusing to follow the pair of women through the census years and to see how they could never quite decide how old they were – vain to the last?

Robert Snooks

There is a connection between the Pages at the King's Arms and a marker stone to be found on the moor at Boxmoor, in the parish of Northchurch between Berkhamsted and Hemel Hempstead. The stone commemorates the death by hanging of Robert (otherwise called James) Snooks. It was placed there in 1904 but the deed for which Snooks lost his life took place on 10 May 1801, somewhere in this locality.

Some accounts say that Snooks worked for a time as an ostler at the King's Arms. If so, he would have become familiar with the movements of the postboy and with the sight of the bulging postbags he carried. Other accounts have him as a man with a criminal background simply on the lookout for an opportunity to steal. Whatever the case, one night he waited on the moor for John Stevens, the postboy, to pass by on his way to Hemel Hempstead from Tring, held him up and threatened his life, and relieved him of six mailbags containing a very large amount of money, including £50 notes.

While Snooks fled with the booty towards London, leaving a trail of opened bags behind him and mounted on a 'dark-coloured grey horse', John Stevens headed back to the King's Arms to raise the alarm and tell John Page what had happened.

In May 1801 a report appeared in the *London Chronicle*: 'There is great reason to suspect that one James Snooks committed the robbery. He is a native of

Snooks' grave lies on what was lonely moorland but is today sandwiched between two busy roads: the marker is the white stone in the distance.

Hungerford, where his father now resides, is between 30 and 40 years of age, 5 feet 10 or 11 inches high, has light brown hair cut short, is pitted with the small pox, has lived in and about Mary-le-bone, and is well known in the neighbourhood of Portland Place. He left his lodging at No. 3, in Woodstock Street, Mary-le-bone, early on Saturday morning, and was then dressed in a blue coat, with black velvet collar, marcella waistcoat, with blue and white stripes, velveteen breeches, and dark-coloured stockings. He was tried at the Old Bailey about a year ago, for horse stealing and acquitted. He is supposed to have in his possession several Bank of England notes, Aylesbury, High Wycombe, Uxbridge, Stony Stratford, and Banbury notes.'

In due course Snooks was arrested, having tried to spend one of the £50 notes. He stood trial at Hertford Assizes in 1802, was sentenced on a Monday and the sentence of death was carried out on the Thursday following. John Page, as High Constable, oversaw the bringing of the criminal from Hertford prison to Boxmoor, where he was hanged from a tree off the back of a cart. His body was then thrown into the waiting grave, with no ceremony. Snooks is apparently the last man in England to have been hanged and buried at the scene of his crime.

BRAUGHING

Mathew Wall – a second chance at life

Walk down the grass path through the churchyard from The Street, towards the church of St Mary the Virgin at Braughing and you will see to the right a large and quite new headstone with the simple words: 'Mathew [sic] Wall, died 1595'. This is the grave of the 'Old Man' of Braughing, who 'died' and came to life again.

Mathew Wall was the son of a local farmer at Green End and, as a young man, suffered an illness that caused him to fall into a trance-like sleep so deep that he was believed to have died. His body was prepared for burial and placed

Mathew Wall's grave is marked by a new headstone.

in a coffin, and on the day fixed for his funeral, 2 October, it was carried from his home to the churchyard. The last part of the journey was along Fleece Lane, which was little more than a footpath that ran from the corner of the Golden Fleece inn yard to the church. Being early autumn, it was lightly covered with fallen leaves and one of the bearers suddenly slipped and fell. The coffin was unceremoniously banged on the ground. Then, while the bearers and mourners recovered themselves, they heard knocking coming from inside the coffin.

It was probably with some trepidation that the lid of the coffin was levered off, but fear must have turned rapidly to joy when they found Mathew alive and conscious once more. He was whisked home and nursed back to health, and the following spring he married the girl who thought she'd lost him forever. They went on to have a family and Mathew died in the fullness of time and was, finally, buried here in the churchyard, having been given a second chance at life.

It sounds like a fable or fairy story, but there is documentary evidence that it is in fact true. In his lifetime Mathew must have been the object of much curiosity and the story would have been told and retold locally. In his will, he ensured that it would not be forgotten. Among other detailed provisions, he left money to be paid to the sexton to look after his grave and each year on 2 October to ring the church bells; 'a poor man' was also to be paid to sweep Fleece Lane free of leaves each autumn (although considering the useful role leaves played in his release, that seems a little perverse!).

The directions were followed and, for over 400 years, Braughing villagers have remembered the 'Old Man' and his tale. The church bells are rung on 2 October, first tolled as they would have been as his coffin approached down Fleece Lane, then switching to a wedding peal in happiness and relief. In a remarkable instance of continuity, sweeping the lane and caring for the grave was undertaken for almost 200 years until the mid-20th century by members of the Drage family, who filled the post of sexton for generations.

In 1951 Dora Fry and Claud Eastwall wrote in *Herts Countryside* magazine that 'the "Old Man's" grave is always lovingly tended; briar and rambling roses smile on the last earthly remains of a happy farmer of Braughing in Queen Elizabeth's days.' The roses have gone, but the new stone was donated in 2001 and Mathew Wall's legacy lives on.

CHESHUNT

LADY MEUX – RAGS TO RICHES

The Meux family vault in Cheshunt churchyard, tight against the church wall and surrounded by iron railings, is hardly a thing of romance, but the story of Valerie Susie Meux, née Langdon (or perhaps Reece), is certainly fit for a romantic novel.

Although perhaps 'rags' is an exaggeration for her early life, she certainly came from a lowly background as actress and barmaid, to become one of the richest women in England. After her husband's death in 1900, she had an income reckoned at about £50,000 per annum (very roughly worth nearly £2 million today), while her properties included Dauntsey House in Wiltshire, a town house in Park Lane, a chateau at Sucy en Brie, Sheen House at East Sheen and, of course, Theobald's Park here in Hertfordshire.

She married Henry Bruce Meux in 1878 and he lavished money and jewellery on his lovely wife. He was the owner of the successful Horseshoe Brewery, heir to a baronetcy and a huge family fortune. She was beautiful, determined and obviously highly intelligent for she took to the high life with enthusiasm and energy. Within five years, Henry had succeeded to the baronetcy after the death of his father and the young couple were looking for a house and estate within easy reach of London that they could make their own. They found it at Theobald's Park, a family property that had been out of use for some time and neglected, and the new Lady Meux began to create an impressive country estate.

The house at Theobald's was enlarged and modernised and for the grounds she designed and had built a swimming pool, a Turkish bath, a racquet court, a roller skating rink, a menagerie, and a museum for her Egyptian relics, including several mummies. The honeymoon had been spent in Egypt and was the start of an abiding interest in Egyptology. She also took a keen interest in breeding racehorses at the Theobald's stud, including the Derby winner, *Volodyovski*, in 1901.

After Henry's early death in 1900 at the age of 43, Lady Meux continued to take a full interest in the running of the Meux brewery. For many years she was the largest shareholder, and until 1902 all the directors were her nominees. Yet, in true romantic style, although she was one of the richest women in England

and could count Edward VII, among others, as a guest at her dinners, she could not break into 'polite' society – Victorian or Edwardian – or melt the Meux family's hearts towards her.

Perhaps one of the most remarkable of her actions was to bring the dismantled Temple Bar from London to Theobald's. Designed by Sir Christopher Wren and once a landmark at the end of the Strand, it had been taken down in 1878 when the area was cleared for the new Royal Courts of Justice and had lain in pieces ever since. Her obituary in *The Times* states that the City of London Corporation gave it to Sir Henry, rather than any money changing hands. The Bar was brought to Hertfordshire over a period beginning in 1887, a huge undertaking, and re-erected as the impressive main entrance on the carriageway to the house. In more recent years its state of dilapidated neglect caused much concern, but today it is back in London, where it was re-erected in 2004, this time at the entrance to Paternoster Square.

Lady Meux died on 20 December 1910 and was buried here in the Meux vault. Having no children, she left most of her fortune to her friend, Vice Admiral the Hon Sir Hedworth Lambton on condition he changed his name to Meux, which he subsequently did. Her 'famous jewels', including spectacular ropes of pearls, she left to Lady Lambton, her Egyptian relics to the British Museum.

Lady Meux is buried in the Meux family vault.

CODICOTE

John Gootheridge – buried twice

In Memory of John Gootheridge
Who Died October 30th 1824. In The 79th Year of His Age.
Reburied a Week Later.

The white-painted wooden graveboard, easily located by the path to the side of the church, has clearly been restored since it was originally raised. These wooden boards were once common, and a surprising number do survive, but most have rotted away over the centuries – this one, however, first restored in 1921, has a certain curiosity value!

The bare facts are recorded in the parish burial register: '1824, November 4th, John Gootheridge, of Knebworth, aged 79 years. This poor Gootheridge,

The restored graveboard that tells the tale of John Gootheridge.

a worthy old man and formerly a farmer, and the Vicar's churchwarden, was taken out of his grave by some "Resurrection-men" nearly a week after interment. They left the corpse upon the grass (being disturbed by some unknown cause) where it was found; it was then re-interred; a great sensation, of course, took place in the parish.'

The *County Chronicle* has a little more: 'Some of those pests of society, called resurrection men, one night last week paid a visit to the church at Coddicote [sic]...The wretches took the body out of the coffin, and dragged it some distance in the churchyard, when in consequence of hearing the report of two guns, supposed to have been fired by some poachers in the neighbourhood, the fellows made their escape, and left the corpse in the church-yard...'. In 1921, when the graveboard was being replaced, the *Hertfordshire News* (19 April) came up with some supplementary information from 'our Codicote correspondent' – 'a shepherd, named Martin, had an alarming experience as the result of the raiders' gruesome exploit. Martin, it is stated, was crossing the churchyard on his way to the sheep meadows of Mansell's Farm, when he fell over John Gootheridge's corpse. According to the village story, Martin was very much scared and raised an alarm.' As well he might!

Gootheridge was the victim of grave robbers, also called amongst other things resurrection men or sack-em-up men or bodysnatchers. Had they not been interrupted at their horrible work the body would soon have been on its way to London and the anatomist's knife; his teeth (if he still had any at his age) would have been sold separately to a dentist to create false teeth for some wealthy patient. Grave robbing was a very lucrative trade by the early 19th century for the strong-stomached and unprincipled. The only way at that time for schools of anatomy to get fresh bodies on which student surgeons could practise was by the back door, literally, and as the number of medical schools increased, so did the demand. Only the bodies of executed criminals could legally be made available for dissection and despite the many petty crimes for which people could be hanged in those days, there were never enough to guarantee supply.

Case after case of bodysnatching made the newspapers all over the country and there were several incidents in Hertfordshire. Relatives resorted to keeping watch over their recently buried loved ones at night. Some parishes built special little watch houses in the churchyard, or paid a local man as a kind of security guard for the dead. The graverobbers would keep their own watch on churchyards, and working in pairs or small groups come in at dead of night to remove new corpses. They usually worked carefully so as not to disturb the ground too much and it is impossible to estimate for certain how many bodies were removed from their graves in this way.

By the 1830s a resurrectionist could make up to 10 guineas for a corpse in good condition at the London schools, which was a huge sum in relation to a labourer's wage. They took nothing but the naked body, since exhumation itself was not against the law and a dead body was not real property – but the shroud and coffin were real property so they could be hanged for taking those!

Once they had made off with the body they would have to move fairly quickly to get it to London. The year before Gootheridge died, in 1823, two robbers had miscalculated the timing when they took the body of William Gilman from Luton churchyard and drove it on a cart along the road through Harpenden and St Albans – the offensive smell raised suspicions and the two were apprehended.

The beginning of the end for the trade came when the infamous duo Burke and Hare were caught in Edinburgh providing fresh corpses by murder. In 1831 a group of 'Burkers' were caught in London: three men who were estimated to have disposed of over a thousand corpses. This was the final straw for an appalled public and a year later the Anatomy Act was passed, which allowed people to leave their bodies for dissection and also medical schools to use the unclaimed bodies of paupers who died in the workhouse. Sadly, this solution only created more horror stories to chill the blood of the elderly poor!

DIGSWELL

KIT NASH – POACHER

'Kit' (Caroline) Nash was a true rural character, though perhaps better as someone else's neighbour than your own! Born in 1849, the illegitimate daughter of Sarah Nash, she lived all her life in a cottage at Harmer Green, on the corner between the bridleway and the lane. The cottage has long since been demolished but it is remembered in the name of a house, Kit's Corner.

She was an imposing woman, over 6 ft tall, who smoked a clay pipe and usually wore a battered old hat, sacks tied round her waist as an apron, and big men's boots. She often carried a gun and wasn't slow to threaten to use it – and did! Kit was notorious in the district as a female poacher. An advantage of the voluminous skirts she wore was that they were ideal for hiding rabbits and other game, and stolen vegetables, from gamekeepers and policemen. Few were brave enough to search her, though they all knew what she got up to.

Kit was, however, no stranger to the courts. The calendar of prisoners for the Winter Assize in 1887 lists eighteen convictions for her since 1865: six for assaults, two for damage, three under the Game Laws, three for stealing food, two for drunkenness, one for wounding a dog, and one for shooting. For the latter – 'shooting with intent' at Police Constable Summerling in 1873 – she had been sentenced to five years' penal servitude. That year, 1887, she was before the Assize judges for stealing grain, and got nine months' hard labour. One of her three children, Valentine, was even born inside Her Majesty's Prison, St Albans, in 1888.

Kit was married for a time to John Darnell of Tewin, a ne'er-do-well who fitted right in with her lifestyle. In 1882 they had both been in trouble. One January day PC Hart had suspected Darnell of stealing turnips and stopped his cart between Tewin and Burnham Green. When the constable tried to search the cart, Darnell hit him with a stick and 'threatened to blow his brains out'. Later three policemen, comprising an inspector and two sergeants (one of the latter being the same Summerling who had already faced Kit's gun) arrived at Kit's cottage to arrest Darnell. They were confronted by Kit armed with a billhook and threatening to 'chop down the first one who came near her' – then she went for her gun. Luckily she was overpowered before she could get off a shot, and not surprisingly she and Darnell were convicted of assaulting the police, and back to prison went Kit. Not long after that, Darnell disappeared from her life.

Undeniably she had a great affinity with the natural world around her, as all great poachers have. And despite her fearsome reputation, in later life she attracted some influential friends. Lady Cowper was a visitor from Panshanger, and more locally Mrs Rose of Highfield (the Roses of Rose's Lime Juice fame) sent meals to Kit's cottage every day from her own kitchen, carried over by the maid.

Her uncompromising independence continued to the end of her life. When she became almost blind, she found her way about her garden by means of a rope she had plaited herself from long grass. She liked to sit in her front garden and listen to the world around her, recognising people by their footsteps. Even then

The grave of Caroline Darnell, otherwise known as Kit Nash.

she kept a grip on her gun, and once during the First World War years fired blind into her fruit trees when she thought soldiers had got in and were 'scrumping'.

Eventually old age got the better of her and Kit was taken to Hatfield Workhouse, where she died on 9 October 1930, aged 81. As the verse on her gravestone reminds us:

Not the righteous, not the righteous,
Sinners Jesus came to call.

EAST BARNET

MEASURING STARS AND OPENING PEWS

John Hadley – Measuring the stars

There is little to indicate that the man commemorated on his gravestone as 'John Hadley, of East Barnet, Esq, dyed the 14th February 1743 aged 61 years' was a major figure in early 18th-century scientific discovery, taking a prominent part in the quest to conquer the problem of accurately calculating longitude at sea. John Hadley invented, amongst other things, the octant, which was the predecessor of the sextant.

John Hadley's chest tomb.

The Hadley family lived at the house called Ussage (or Osidge) in East Barnet and John's father George was High Sheriff of Hertfordshire when John was only nine years old. John took a great interest in his locality and was a governor of Barnet grammar school from 1720. He inherited the estate, plus other land, when George died in 1729. He was therefore financially secure and could afford to devote time and money to his scientific interests, together with his two brothers George and Henry (in fact, George became famous in his own right as the meteorologist who explained the working of the Trade Winds, another vital subject for those at sea).

John's first great invention was the reflector telescope, an improvement on Isaac Newton's initial design. The concept depended on the use of two mirrors, one with a hole in it so that light could reach the eyepiece. Newton had not been able to produce a clear enough surface on the mirrors to allow him to see the heavens distinctly. By meticulously grinding and polishing the mirror surface, the Hadley brothers finally produced a telescope that impressed the Royal Society in 1721 and, when given to Edmund Halley to 'test drive', enabled him to see details on the surfaces of Jupiter and Saturn. An added and equally welcome innovation was that Hadley's telescope was only 6 ft long and could be moved easily, as opposed to the 123 ft long telescope of Christopher Huygens that was in use at the time.

With that success under his belt, John turned his attention to the problem of determining longitude at sea. In 1707 there had been terrible loss of life off the Scilly Isles with the wreck of the fleet under the command of Sir Cloudesley Shovell, due to the navigators mistaking their position. It had forced Parliament to announce a monetary reward for whoever could prove they had a solution that would define longitude to within one degree – without that knowledge anyone navigating at sea could easily drift off course and be lost. In 1731 John Hadley presented the Royal Society with his octant, which could measure the altitude of the stars or the sun above the horizon even when a ship was rolling – if the accurate time was also known, longitude could be calculated with confidence (as Dava Sobel's book *Longitude* about the clockmaker John Harrison relates). There had been other instruments in use, but the octant was very accurate and could be used day or night. In fact, the design was so good that even when the sextant came into use from the late 1760s many ships continued to use the octant, well into the 19th century.

John married Elizabeth Hodges in 1734 and they had one son. After John's death in 1744, the family home Ussage was pulled down and his son gradually frittered away both property and money, but John Hadley's true beneficiaries were men and women at sea.

Elizabeth Press; a quiet life.
(see next page)

Elizabeth Press – Pew opener

If John Hadley touched the world, Elizabeth Press by contrast lived in a very restricted circle, but in her way she made her own mark. She is buried by the church path and her gravestone records that she was 'for many years a pew opener of this church' when she died aged 80 in 1877. Pew openers were the mainstay of church life before the enclosed pews were ripped out in the Victorian era and beyond. Elizabeth would have opened the door to the pew and ushered in the occupants before each service, and each pew was the jealously guarded property of a certain individual or family. In many churches, 'pew rent' was paid each year and woe betide anyone who tried to sit somewhere they shouldn't!

ESSENDON

Fear in the Night

Frances and Eleanor Bamford – Victims of the 'Zep'

As you walk past the church from the lychgate, stop to read the stone plaque on the wall that records the events of the night of Sunday, 3 September 1916, when Frances Bamford, aged 26, and her 12-year-old sister Eleanor were killed, 'sacrificed in the course of a Zeppelin raid over this church and village' as the inscription has it, and the church bombed. The headstone that marks their grave is further down the churchyard, on the left-hand side, and it tells more of the story.

During the First World War, towns and villages in England got their first experience of aerial bombardment,

Frances and Eleanor Bamford, killed by a Zeppelin bomb.

initally from airships and Zeppelins, and then from aeroplanes. The east coast suffered badly, because to bombs dropped from the air were added shells fired from German vessels in the North Sea, but London was a major target and the course steered by the enemy airships was frequently over Hertfordshire, coming in from the east and silently approaching the capital. Just as in the Second World War, bombs not dropped on the primary target were often jettisoned at random over defenceless villages on the way back.

In the early hours of that September morning (the church clock stopped at 2.23 am) over 20 bombs fell on this quiet little village. Most fell harmlessly on open ground but the vestry of the church took a direct hit, the lodge and two other cottages were destroyed, and many windows in the village were shattered.

The Bamford family lived in a cottage about 50 yards from the church. Their neighbour later told the local newspaper that when she heard the Zeppelins overhead she immediately began to get her eight children downstairs. 'I heard Fanny (the elder girl) call out, "Come down to the Grove, Mrs –". I was about to join her when something seemed to tell me not to, and I turned instead up the entry leading from the back of our house to the front, accompanied by my children. At that very moment a bomb dropped right by Fanny and her sister. Fanny, poor girl, was struck in the stomach and killed outright; her sister Eleanor had her right leg smashed. It was awful. We ran about the street, not knowing where to go.'

It isn't difficult to imagine the sheer horror of that night. As the old couple in the Lodge said, 'We were nearly frit to death in the pitch dark and all.' The two cottages destroyed were lived in by two elderly widows, who lost everything. One of them was distraught at the loss of photographs of her five sons – four of them at the Front in France and one already a casualty of the war.

Apparently the Bamford family had gone to shelter in a grove of trees about 400 yards behind their cottage. Only Frances and Eleanor had hesitated for some reason and had not reached the trees before the bombs fell. Eleanor died of her injuries soon after.

The village was besieged by hundreds of curious spectators in the days after the raid. Local people and visitors lined the route to the church for the girls' funeral, watching silently as the two oak coffins were carried past on hand biers, covered with flowers. The church was still a mass of rubble and broken glass but the service was held at the west end. Afterwards the girls were buried, and 'many of the villagers and general public filed past the burial place, and then slowly and reverently the crowd dispersed.'

Reverend Robert Orme – Afraid of burial alive

The very plain tomb hard up against the churchyard boundary to the left as you walk towards the church porch would not catch your eye unless you knew the strange story of the Reverend Robert Orme, Rector of Essendon for 52 years, who died aged 83, in 1843. He suffered a fear of being buried alive and made arrangements against that terrible possibility.

His tomb was to be above ground, with a lockable steel door at one end and the key to it left in his hand as he was placed in his coffin. Some bread and wine were to accompany him to the grave also, in case he needed sustenance before he could get out.

Many people must have suffered this dread over the centuries, but it was the Victorians in particular whose spines tingled at the thought, probably exacerbated

The tomb of the Reverend Orme.

by Gothic horror tales. Edgar Allan Poe's *Fall of the House of Usher* has a particularly worrying description of deep scratch marks on the inside of the coffin lid! Ideas put forward to avoid waking underground and being unable to get out included placing a cord in the hands of the deceased, which was attached to a bell above ground that could then be rung to attract notice. It was not an idle fear, of course, because with no way to monitor feeble life signs in people suffering coma it would be all too easy for someone to be pronounced dead before their time (see the story of Mathew Wall in Braughing).

The end of the tomb is slightly askew, but do not fear, Reverend Orme had no need to fight his way out!

GREAT AMWELL

FIRE AND WATER

Harold Abrahams

The title sequence of the 1981 film *Chariots of Fire* has become one of those iconic movie moments – white-clad young men running in slow motion through the surf along an otherwise deserted beach, accompanied by the music of Vangelis. The film told the story of the 1924 Olympic Games and, particularly, the part played by two of those young men – Harold Abrahams and Eric Liddell. Harold Abrahams, the first Englishman to win an Olympic gold medal for the 100 metre sprint, lies here in the leafy churchyard of St John the Baptist beneath a simple headstone close to the curve of the church wall.

Abrahams, born in Bedford, came from a sporting family – his brothers Sir

Harold Abrahams' headstone,
by the church wall.

HERTFORDSHIRE Who Lies Beneath?

Sidney Abrahams and Sir Adolphe Abrahams were both athletes and the latter was involved in the development of British sports medicine – and he used his time at Cambridge University to pursue his athletic dreams, excelling at the long jump and sprinting. He represented Britain at the 1920 Olympics but on that occasion did little to highlight his talents in the 100 and 200 metres, long jump and relay race. Three years later, however, he set a British long jump record at 23 ft 8¾ inches, and now his hunger for success was focused on the 1924 Olympic Games in Paris.

In the days when amateur sport meant just that, he went so far as to employ a professional coach, Sam Mussabini, which was as much a matter for comment and disapproval in the 'establishment' as his Jewish background (he converted to Roman Catholicism in 1934). It paid off, as he began to excel at the '100 metres dash' and pushed the long jump record to 24 ft 2½ inches, where it stayed for the next 32 years.

At the Olympic Games in 1924, everything came together for a magnificent British victory over the confident American sprinters. Nailing his colours to the mast, in the second heat Abrahams set a British and Olympic record for the 100 metres, at 10.6 seconds. Then, to show it wasn't just a flash in the pan, he equalled the record in the semi-finals. And again in the final, when he beat the American favourite, Jackson Scholz, by two feet at the tape. It was to be another 44 years before we produced another such champion – Linford Christie in 1968.

Abrahams also reached the final of the 200 metres, but could not repeat his success and came last, with Scholz this time powering to victory. He did, though, run with the relay team that took the silver medal and set a British record time of 41.2 seconds, not shattered until 1952.

We're so used to the lengthy medal ceremonies at today's Olympic Games that it comes as amusing light relief to discover that in 1924 there were no presentations at all, and Harold Abrahams had to wait for the postman to deliver his medals – and to pay excess postage on the package!

Sad to relate, 1924 was the height and close to the end of Harold Abraham's sporting career, cut prematurely short the next year by a leg injury while long jumping. However, although he went back to his profession as a solicitor, he stayed prominent in the sporting world, writing and broadcasting, and becoming involved in several sporting bodies, notably the Amateur Athletic Association and British Amateur Athletic Association (BAAA), of which he was appointed Chairman in 1963. His only recognition from the establishment, however, was not for his sporting achievements, on the field and off, but a CBE for his work with the National Parks Commission, in 1957.

It's a nice touch to the story that every year after that 1924 victory – on 7 July at exactly 7 pm – Harold Abrahams dined with Arthur Porritt, who had come third in Bronze position in the 100 metres and who was later to become Governor-General of New Zealand and Surgeon to the Royal Family from 1936-67.

Abrahams died on 14 January 1978, aged 78 and is buried here with his wife, Sybil, an opera singer with the D'Oyly Carte Opera Company. He lived for many years in Hertfordshire, at Rickmansworth, Hoddesdon and Great Amwell, and they both took a keen interest in the East Herts Operatic Society.

Robert Mylne

The neat mausoleum of the Mylne family is opposite Harold Abrahams' headstone. It carries memorial inscriptions for several members of the family from the 18th and 19th centuries, not all of whom are actually buried here.

The patriarch of the clan was Robert Mylne (1733-1811), 'Architect and Engineer, FRS'. The detail of his life's work makes fascinating reading:

'A native of Edinburgh (and lineal descendant by birth and profession of John Mylne, Master Mason to King James the Third of Scotland) ... He designed and constructed the magnificent Bridge of Blackfriars, London. From the year 1762 he was Engineer to the New River Aqueduct. And from the same period had the superintendence of the Cathedral Church of St Paul as Architect and Paymaster of the works. And dying in London his remains were interred near to those of Sir Christopher Wren, in the vaults of that Cathedral.'

The bridge he built at Blackfriars was the first on that spot across the Thames, constructed over the period 1760 to 1769. Officially it was called 'William Pitt Bridge', but popular usage renamed it simply 'Blackfriars', and until the 1780s it was a toll bridge, charging to cross the river. It had nine arches of Portland stone and looked very different to its replacement a hundred years later, with its five wrought-iron arches.

The New River was part of the water supply to London, created at the beginning of the 17th century by cutting a channel from Amwell and Chadwell

The Mylne mausoleum is topped by a decorative urn.

in Hertfordshire into the capital – the churchyard overlooks the springs from which it drew its water. It flowed from here into Clerkenwell, and then continued the journey to its customers through wooden pipes. The New River Company was a commercial venture that charged customers for the water they received, so only wealthy Londoners had the benefit of Hertfordshire spring water. Having said that, the water was far from pure and in the early 19th century was found to be polluted by sewage. The Company operated until 1904, when it was taken over by the Metropolitan Water Board.

Robert Mylne's involvement with the New River was continued by his son, William Chadwell Mylne (1781–1863), who, as the inscription on the mausoleum wall says, 'For upward of half a century had the care and management of the works of the New River'. One of his achievements was the design of a new gauge to limit the amount of water taken from the Lea after that river was joined by a channel with the New River to increase the water supply. His father had designed a gauge in 1770, 'enclosed in a massive marble chest like a sarcophagus', but William's in 1856 depended on two iron boats floating on the Lea, the rise and fall of which controlled the amount of water let through the sluice gate. The historian W. Branch Johnson, in *The Industrial Archaeology of Hertfordshire* (1970), describes the system and also points out that William designed the earliest surviving pumping station in the county, at Amwell Hill.

Before leaving the mausoleum, Robert's wife Mary deserves a mention too. She had as busy a life as her husband and son, though in a domestic role: she had ten children, and died at the early age of 49 in 1797. Her children dedicated the monument to her:

'A warm heart, and accurate judgement
Engaging wit and lively humour'

HARPENDEN

VILLAIN OF THE DREYFUS CASE

Count de Voilemont (Baron de Esterhazy)

A very shady character indeed lies here, beneath the assumed name of 'Count de Voilemont' but who is actually Charles Marie Ferdinand Walsin Esterhazy, otherwise known as the Baron de Esterhazy. He was deeply involved in the shameful Dreyfus case that caused uproar in France in the late 19th century – in fact, he was the villain of the piece.

Esterhazy had an uninspiring career in the French army from the 1860s; he worked at times for military intelligence but by the 1890s he was in desperate straits, deeply in debt as he spent whatever money he could get his hands on –

by fair means or foul – on a life of ease, gambling and dissipation. He became increasingly bitter against the army authorities whom he felt had not recognised his talents, despite the fact that his life was built on lies: he was not entitled to the titles he claimed, and he had had no compunction about falsifying his army records to present himself in a heroic light.

One talent that he did have was to be fluent in the German language and he began to trade information with the German military authorities, including details of new developments in French artillery. Hostility and mutual suspicion

The now almost indecipherable headstone of the traitorous Count.

rumbled on between France and Germany during the 19th century, and the Franco-Prussian War was only brought to an end by the Treaty of Frankfurt in 1871; Esterhazy's espionage was therefore an extremely serious, and traitorous, matter.

In 1894, when a scapegoat had to be found for the leaks coming from the French side, a 35-year-old Jewish soldier named Captain Alfred Dreyfus was accused of being the spy who had betrayed his country. The 'Dreyfus Affair' had begun.

Dreyfus was convicted at a secret court martial and sent to the notorious prison on Devil's Island, off French Guiana – in effect, a living death. Two years later, evidence began to surface of Esterhazy's guilt but his military superiors protected him, acquitting him in 1898 of all charges in a trial behind closed doors.

It was at this point that the eminent writer Emile Zola wrote his famous work *J'accuse*, accusing the French government and military of anti-semitism and of deliberately sending an innocent man to prison. A huge public row blew up, not only in France but all around the world, but the authorities refused to back down. As a sop to public opinion, in 1899 Dreyfus was brought back from the island to undergo a second court martial and was again found guilty, but with 'extenuating circumstances'. He refused to accept a nominal pardon – 'Liberty is nothing to me without honour.' It wasn't until 1906 that the charges were finally dropped completely.

In the meantime, the evidence of double-dealing, prejudice and sheer stupidity amongst French military commanders had to be got rid of and Esterhazy was paid off with a military pension and the means to go abroad. In September 1898 he came to England and here at Harpenden he lived an obscure life until he died in 1923. The 1911 census records him living at The Elms, Station Road – Count Jean de Voilement, aged 60, describing himself as 'Literary man, Foreign Newspapers and Reviews Correspondent', with a 37-year-old wife and a housekeeper. As his gravestone says:

'He has outsoared the shadow of our night.'

Francis ('Frank') Salisbury

Frank Owen Salisbury was born in Harpenden in 1874, one of twelve children. His father was a 'plumber, decorator and ironmonger' with a shop at Leyton Road, who at one time rather despaired of what course in life his rather delicate little boy would follow.

Frank was educated at home, and then when he was fifteen he was apprenticed to his brother James at his stained-glass works in St Albans. James recognised Frank's talent for drawing and sent him to Heatherley's School of Art in London, a faith that was rewarded when Frank won a five-year scholarship to the Royal Academy Schools. The first portrait he exhibited at the RA was in 1899, of the girl who became his wife, Alice Greenwood.

From that beginning, Salisbury's career went from strength to strength. His main areas of work were in portraiture, religious subjects, and historical and ceremonial events, including war scenes. As a portrait painter he was in demand by some of the best known and most powerful people in the world; in fact he came to be known as 'Britain's Painter Laureate'. Royal subjects included George V, many members of the Royal Family, and the first painting of the new Queen Elizabeth II. He painted Winston Churchill more times than any other artist, two of his famous portraits being *Blood, Sweat and Tears*, and *The Siren Suit*. Other sitters included Prime Minister Herbert Asquith, Pope Pius XII, Benito Mussolini, Montgomery of Alamein, and no fewer than six US Presidents,

Frank Salisbury's grave is marked by a simple, low stone,
to the right of the angel.

including F.D. Roosevelt and Eisenhower. He spent a considerable time in America and enjoyed high success amongst the wealthy families at the peak of industry and finance.

Salisbury became a very wealthy man through his painting. He still kept up an interest in stained-glass, though, and produced work for more homely projects, including the chapel at the former National Children's Home in Harpenden. In 1933 he was elected Master of the Worshipful Company of Glaziers and Painters of Glass. In his private life Salisbury remained a committed Methodist – he paid for the restoration of John Wesley's house in London in 1934.

By the end of his life he was one of the most famous painters in the world and he and his family lived here in Harpenden, first in a house near the church and then at Red Gables, which he had built near Rothamsted and where he died on 31 August 1962.

HATFIELD

John Whitemore – a life in three centuries

St Etheldreda's at Hatfield, just outside the gates of Hatfield House, is one of those churches that it is well worthwhile making a special trip to see inside. The tomb of Robert Cecil, first Secretary of State and Prime Minister to Queen Elizabeth I, is particularly fascinating, with an unnerving carved skeleton beneath his stone effigy, an effective reminder that all pomp and wealth comes to naught in the end. This being the church to the 'big house', there are naturally other well known 'names' here, including Lady Caroline Lamb, who has gone down in history as the girl who loved the 'bad, mad and dangerous to know' Lord Byron rather too well and paid the price with her sanity.

John Whitemore lived through three centuries.

47

But spare a glance, too, for the wooden graveboard just outside the main door into the church. This marks the grave of John Whitemore, who died on 3 December 1801, aged 103 years. Not such a grand age, perhaps, though certainly remarkable, but there is more than a passing interest in the thought that by the time he died this old man had lived through three centuries.

When John Whitemore was born, William III was on the throne and only nine years had passed since the turmoil of James II's reign had ended in the king fleeing to the Continent. It was still less than 40 years since the end of Cromwell's Protectorate and Charles II had brought the monarchy back to London. Only a generation away, his parents and grandparents would have lived through civil war and all the uncertainties that entailed. By the time he died, George III was on the throne, undergoing periods of madness more times than not, and was just being proclaimed King of Great Britain and Ireland – the United Kingdom was born in 1801. Perhaps better not to mention that we had lost the American colonies thirty years before. John would certainly have been aware that by the end of the 1700s we were at war with the French after their Revolution in 1789 – though not that England would soon face its greatest threat of invasion before the Second World War.

The Hatfield he lived in was the largest parish in Hertfordshire, but estimates in 1663 give a population of only 1,710, or about 855 in the town itself. In 1801 the census recorded 2,442, including 1,221 in the town. Still such small numbers, but growing nonetheless. Perhaps the building of the new mill at Mill Green in 1762 was an indicator of increased demand in the area.

In many ways life changed little during the 18th century. There were no trains, of course, in his lifetime, but he would have seen the great age of the stagecoach arrive. Hatfield is on the Great North Road and was a stopping place to change horses and pick up passengers. New turnpike roads had made long-distance travel a little safer and more comfortable, though most roads were still a morass of glutinous mud in winter and choking dust in summer. Many people who, like John Whitemore, lived in an agricultural county went on as their ancestors had done – in the same rhythms of the seasons and not a lot different in the tools they used or the seeds they sowed, marking the passage of time by fairs and markets. The agricultural revolution had not yet touched Hertfordshire to any extent.

Did he feel the pace of progress begin to stir and quicken as he reached the end of his life? Population growth all over the country was beginning to gather strength after the 1780s, and so was the pace of industrialisation, with more and more people moving from the land into urban areas; the England of just another 50 years later would have been unrecognisable to him. Perhaps, after all, a centenarian of the 18th century could have looked back on the last settled period of English history before the oncoming Victorian expansion of industry, science, empire and social strife.

HERTFORD ALL SAINTS

A Maker of Bells and Oriental Masters

John Briant

As a young man growing up in Suffolk in the mid-18th century, John Briant wanted to be a clockmaker and during his apprenticeship he was taught the related arts of chime making and bellfounding. Although he remained a skilled clockmaker all his life, it was with bells that his reputation grew until he was one of the most respected men in his profession.

Born in 1748, he began his working life in St Neots, Cambridgeshire and then moved to Hertford with his father in about 1780. By then he had made his first bell – a clock bell for the house of Quickswood in Clothall. In Hertford he and his father set up a foundry and clock works in Parliament Row and after his father's death in 1785, John took over the running of the business. Over the next four decades Briant's fame spread throughout Hertfordshire and into the neighbouring counties, with commissions coming in from as far afield as Leicester and Rugby. Altogether over 400 bells came out of his Hertford foundry.

He enjoyed the patronage of James Cecil, 6th Earl of Salisbury and his first major contract was to recast the eight bells of St Etheldreda's church at Hatfield in 1786. After that he worked on church bells all over north and east Hertfordshire, including those of St Andrew's and All Saints here in Hertford. Sadly the bells he cast for All Saints were lost when the church suffered a devastating fire in 1891.

The skill required in successful bellfounding was immense. First of all a full-sized scale drawing of the new bell was made, using mathematical tables that accounted for every nuance of tone and dimension. This was used to cut two 'strickle boards' for the outer and inner shape of the bell. Moulds were then made, using clay or loam, dried in huge ovens and 'decorated' with the name of the bell or the founder or some relevant phrase. The outer case fitted over the inner, the hot 'bell metal' of copper and tin was poured into the mould and cast.

After the new bell emerged from its mould, and often when hanging in the church tower, it was worked on by hand, the craftsmen chipping away at the metal on the inside surface until just the right note was achieved. It was intricate and highly-skilled work and Briant was one of the best of his day.

John Briant's gravestone was moved back to its rightful place after protests by local bellringers.

Most bellfounders were also bellringers, and Briant was no exception. How satisfying it must have been to hear a bell you had created yourself ringing out from the church tower.

John Briant retired in 1825, probably because his eyesight was failing, and he sold the business to Thomas Mears at the famous Whitechapel Foundry. To be near his daughter Mary, he moved into the Marlborough Almshouses in St Albans, where he died on 27 February 1829 in his 81st year. His body was brought back to Hertford for burial and, in accordance with his wishes, a gross of iron screws were placed in his coffin to keep him company on the journey.

When the new Gascoyne Way ring road was built in the 1990s, Briant's grave was one of those that had to be moved, as the road cut off part of the old churchyard. However, local bellringers paid to have his stone moved back to its old position and you can find it hard by the wall as you come into the churchyard from the dual carriageway. The inscription had become illegible over time and in 2000 a new stone was placed on the grave; there is also a bronze plaque to his memory inside the church. The stone says simply: 'He was a famous Bellfounder and Clockmaker.'

Meer Abdal Aly Moolavy

Foreign names are not uncommon in churchyards, but the date – 1812 – that goes with this one make it stand out. The inscription reads:

> *Moolavy*
> *Meer Abdal Aly*
> *Native of the City of Lucknow, Capital of the Province of Oude,*
> *Teacher of Oriental Languages in the East India College.*
> *Died 13 October 1812*
> *Aged 39*
> *Erected by the Honble. East India Company as a proof of their esteem.*

Created in 1600, the East India Company was the agent through which the British government ruled India for two and a half centuries. It was established as a trading company but it also ran the local and central administration of that vast country, so that by the beginning of the 19th century it had not only an army but also a merchant shipping fleet and a civil service of its own.

A job in the Company's civil service could be the entry to a profitable career. Appointment to posts was by nomination by the Directors – in other words, who you knew counted for more than what you knew. In 1806 the Company decided to open a college to give entrants a 'finishing' education before they were sent out to India and for a short time it was housed in Hertford Castle. However, in 1809 the college moved to the nearby Haileybury estate and a new purpose-built school.

The young men, aged 16 to 19, were taught a variety of subjects, including law, mathematics, classics and political economy, but perhaps the most useful for their future lives were the Oriental languages that introduced them to a new culture. While the professors were white Englishmen, they were assisted by masters who came from the provinces of India. Stephen Austin, the Hertford

*The row containing the graves of the Oriental masters is overgrown
and the stones have faded considerably.*

printing firm, even had a special department dedicated to publishing Oriental studies.

The East India Company's long reign in India came to an end after the Indian Mutiny in 1857, when the British government stepped in at last to take control, and the college closed. In 1862 Haileybury College opened, this time as a public school.

Next to that of Moolavy is another grave, on which the inscription has long since eroded, but it was recorded in 1830 by Lewis Turnor for his *History of Hertford*. It marks the resting place of another master, Gholaum Hyder who was

The millstones that mark the miller's grave.

'a native of the Province of Bahar and Persian writing master to the East India College'. He died in 1823, aged 47, and the stone was 'erected by the students of the East India College as a testimony of their regard'.

While you're in the churchyard, look for the millstones that mark the graves of Robert Fincher and his wife Elizabeth. Fincher was the town's millwright in the 18th century, dying in 1777 and the great stones are a fitting memorial to a man who would have been one of the important figures in this market town dependent upon agriculture.

HERTINGFORDBURY

MALT AND MASSAGE

Ben Truman

Hertfordshire has a great brewing tradition and at Hertingfordbury, almost hidden beneath a tree in the churchyard, the Truman tomb bears the name of one of the most famous brewers in the country. Benjamin (Ben) Truman was born in 1699 and under his management the Black Eagle Brewery at Stepney in London became a national institution.

Ben took over shares in the family business from his father Joseph and soon showed an aptitude for the trade. He was also quick to take advantage of PR opportunities that fell into his lap! There is a story that in 1737 the Prince of Wales ordered bonfires lit at Carlton House to celebrate the birth of his daughter,

Ben Truman's tomb is almost hidden under the trees.

and four barrels of beer were set out for the crowd to toast her. The London mob who turned up, though, thought the beer was not up to their standards and threw most of it at each other. The Prince tried again the next night, this time with four barrels from brewer Ben Truman, to the great pleasure of the crowd!

It was porter that made Truman's fortune in the 18th century. This dark, strong, bitter beer, first brewed in 1722, was the staple drink in London, and was also at the time the only beer that could be brewed in quantity and kept for a time without deteriorating. Ben Truman built an enormous complex at the Brick Lane brewery, so huge that it was one of the biggest industrial sites in the country in the second half of the century and a magnet for admiring foreign tourists. He was soon one of the finest brewers in the land, vying amongst others with his friend Samuel Whitbread who lived at Essendon Place nearby. Hertfordshire was the main producer of the dark brown malt used for porter.

Ben Truman had an impressive London home in Brick Lane and a country estate at Pope's Manor here at Hertingfordbury, and he spent lavishly on both. He reconstructed Pope's in the Palladian style, though sadly it was demolished in the 19th century after it was acquired by Lord Salisbury – it was said that he did not want such a fine house so close to his own Hatfield House!

Truman was a canny businessman and made several large loans to the Crown, successive monarchs being chronically short of money. When George III came to the throne in 1760, Truman got his reward when he was knighted as one of the premier businessmen in London.

Six years later, he suffered a personal and business setback with the death of his only son, James, who is also buried here. James had been set to take over the brewery from his father and Ben's other child, Frances, could not compensate for the loss. In fact she and her husband and children took almost no interest in the business. When Ben died on 16 March 1780 he appointed James Grant, his Head Clerk, as executor of his will, 'being well persuaded that by a few years more experience he will be well qualified to conduct my Trade upon the same plan it has been carried on for years past ...'. Grant did not let him down and ran the business almost single-handedly for the next ten years until his death.

You can't fault Ben Truman's advice to his grandson, written when he was an old man: '... there can be no other way of raising a great Fortune but by carrying on an Extensive Trade. I must tell you, Young Man, this is not to be obtained without Spirrit [sic] and great Application...'.

Almeric Paget

Wander on down through the churchyard, past the tall winged figure that marks one of the several memorials to members of the Cowper family – lords of the manor –in the church and outside, and towards the far right-hand corner. Here, facing away from the church, is the impressive patterned marble memorial to Pauline Payne Whitney Paget and her husband, Almeric Hugh Paget, 1st Baron Queenborough. Together they were influential in laying the foundations of modern-day physiotherapy, especially in relation to wounded servicemen.

Almeric Paget was born in 1861 and led a colourful early life. Even though he was the youngest son of Lord Alfred Paget, he liked to recall that as a young man he had only £5 in his pocket when he left England for life as a cowboy in the American West. In a few years, though, he had gone from being a cattle rancher to a wealthy industrialist, with interests in coal, iron and steel.

In 1895 he married a New York heiress, Pauline Payne Whitney, and their wedding was attended by the US President, Grover Cleveland. Six years later they moved to England, finally settling here at Hertingfordbury. Almeric took a close interest in politics and was elected Conservative MP for Cambridge from 1910 to 1917.

The First World War began in August 1914 and it was immediately apparent that wounded servicemen in huge numbers – officers and privates – were going to need care and treatment on modern lines. The couple put their wealth and position behind the establishment of the Almeric Paget Massage Corps – at that time an innovation in care but which had such impressive results that it was in time recognised by the War Office. It was renamed the Almeric Paget Military

The memorial to Pauline, wife of Almeric Paget.

Massage Corps in 1916, and again renamed as the Military Massage Service in 1919. From an initial appointment of 50 masseuses, about 2,000 had been employed by 1919, serving here and overseas. Clinics were opened in hospitals in the UK, as well as a Massage and Electrical Outpatient Clinic at Portland Place in London – it is reckoned that this clinic alone treated some 200 servicemen each day of the war.

Pauline Paget died on 22 November 1916 and this tomb, with her name carved in contrasting marble, was erected by her husband. Five years later, now 1st Baron Queenborough, Almeric Paget remarried and moved to Camfield Place, near Hatfield. Although he remained a public figure, his life in the 1930s was marred by an admiration for General Franco and Adolf Hitler that he shared with several other members of the aristocracy, and royalty. His second marriage ended in divorce and when he died in 1949, Almeric Paget was buried here with Pauline.

KINGS WALDEN

CHARLES DINES – FAITHFUL SERVANT

Parts of the lovely little churchyard at Kings Walden are left to grow wild in the summer months, so it may prove difficult to find the gravestone that marks the resting place of Charles Dines. As you walk towards the church from the lychgate, it is in the area of long grass to the left of the path, near the tree.

In fact, the headstone that stands here is not the one that was originally erected after Charles Dines' death in 1815. Luckily, William B. Gerish recorded the inscriptions at Kings Walden, as he did in most churchyards throughout the county, in the early 20th century and so we have a record of what has now gone.

The original inscription read:

'Sacred to the memory of Charles Dines, gamekeeper to Samuel Whitbread Esq., of Southill, who was attacked by a gang of poachers whilst endeavouring, as a faithful servant, to protect his master's property, and was most inhumanly murdered by one of them on the night of the 9th December 1815, aged 33 years.

Kings Walden churchyard; the Dines grave is to the left of the path.

'The perpetrator of the above horrid act, having violated the Commandment of God, and the Laws of his country suffered the punishment due to his crime. He was executed at Bedford on the 11th day of March 1816.

'This stone is erected at the request of a disconsolate widow, who, with a family, is left to lament the loss of an affectionate husband and truly kind father.'

The game laws of England were severe and landowners often went to great lengths to protect the birds and rabbits on their estates. There was a property qualification for taking game, set in 1671: you had to own property worth £100 p.a., or lease land worth £150. Anyone who could not gain a licence, which meant most of the population, was deemed a poacher if they so much as picked up a dead rabbit along the hedgeside – and temptation could be strong at times of poor harvests when families were going hungry. Penalties could be severe, and became more harsh at the beginning of the 19th century. Carrying a gun and resisting arrest would get a man the death penalty by 1803, and in 1817 simply being caught poaching at night when armed, even if the gun was not used, would mean seven years' transportation to Australia.

There were several cases in Hertfordshire of armed poachers shooting gamekeepers, sometimes fatally. These gangs were feared, not without cause, as it was felt that they would shoot without compunction at men who were simply doing their duty. At this time, too, there was no established police force – the gamekeepers were in effect upholding the law on their patch of land, no matter how unjust that law. The 'perpetrator' in the case of Charles Dines was a man named Edward Chamberlain, who did indeed pay the price for his crime at Bedford on that date.

LANGLEYBURY

AN AMATEUR STAGECOACH DRIVER AND A FAMOUS EXPLORER

William Rudston Faulconer

Just a few yards from the busy dual carriageway, the A41 Watford road, at Hunton Bridge, a tall gravestone catches the eye in the row by the hedge – and yes, it is an old milestone. It once stood beside the road to Brighton and it marks the grave of an enthusiastic amateur stagecoach driver, William Rudston Faulconer.

Faulconer died in 1928, aged 79, and in his professional life was a member of the Stock Exchange. He lived at Abbots Langley and was well known in hunting and sporting circles in the county. His passion, however, was the stagecoach.

The coming of the railways in the first half of the 19th century had effectively killed the stagecoach as a commercial form of transport but services never totally disappeared and in the 1870s and 1880s stagecoach travel was revived by the patronage of wealthy men who fancied themselves seated on the box, whip in hand, and who were usually able to afford to ignore the liabilities of their hobby – there was a romance about it that more than compensated for financial loss. The *Telegraph* to Hertford and the *Wonder* to St Albans were two such latecomers to the road.

In 1898 *The Times* reported the start of the 'coaching season' on 2 May and looked back over the past few decades of the sport: 'Some years ago, when road coaching was revived after the railways had seemingly extinguished it, the proprietors were all men of position who were quite indifferent as to the financial result of their enterprise ... But they have, one after the other, died or abandoned their interest in the road, their places being for the most part taken by the livery stable keepers and professional coachmen.' These, it went on, could make their venture pay by getting subscribers 'willing to pay for the privilege of driving once or twice a week, and it is only so long

A milestone marks the grave of the amateur stagecoach driver.

as a sufficient number of these can be obtained that the coach will be kept on the road.'

Faulconer certainly did not become indifferent to his hobby, and coaching went on for a remarkably long time. There was still a 'coaching season' up to the 1930s in some places: in May 1929 the start of the service between London and Oxford, and London and Windsor was announced.

Faulconer was greatly respected amongst this fraternity. In 1888 when the funeral of James Selby, the hugely popular driver of the *Old Times* coach, took place at Highgate Cemetery, Faulconer was chosen to drive the *Old Times* itself, at the head of a mile-long coach procession (before his death Selby had just set the record for the London to Brighton run at 7 hours 50 minutes and that day all the omnibus and cab drivers in the West End of London appeared with mourning crape bows on their whips). Faulconer reckoned that over the years he drove more than 60 coaches on runs from London, and in May 1927 at the opening meet of the Coaching Club in Hyde Park he was guest of honour as 'senior among amateur coachmen'.

At least he didn't live to see his grand hobby brought to an end, as more and more coaches and equipment were auctioned off as curiosities and mementoes. The record-breaking *Old Times* stagecoach changed hands more than once, but in 1934 it was sold at auction to Bertram Mills, of circus fame.

Violet Cressy-Marcks

Forest and Ocean are children's names unusual enough to make you stop and wonder. The tomb of Francis Fisher records him as the father of the pair, and

The imposing tomb of Francis Fisher.

the husband of 'Violet Olivia', and a little research has opened up a world of early 20th-century exploration and, perhaps, espionage.

Their mother, born in 1895, was Violet Olivia Cressy-Marcks, an intrepid and seemingly tireless traveller, writer, archaeologist, photographer, and maybe spy. Born Violet Rutley, she married Maurice Cressy-Marcks in 1917 but later divorced him, marrying Francis Fisher in 1931. She had one son, William, by her first husband and two more – Ocean and Forest – by her second. As Mrs Fisher she lived at Hazelwood House in King's Langley. However, she was probably away from home more often than she was there.

Ocean and Forest were christened here at Langleybury – one of little Ocean's godfathers in 1933 was the son of Theodore Roosevelt and among those who came to the reception afterwards was the Minister for Saudi Arabia.

The list of Cressy-Marcks' expeditions makes quite exhausting reading. When she was elected to the Royal Geographical Society in 1922 it was said that already she had travelled from Alaska to Java and penetrated the mysteries of Tibet and Kashmiri, and by the 1950s she had circumnavigated the world eight times, gone overland across Africa from Egypt to the Cape, spent nine months on a journey from Lapland to Baluchistan, made six expeditions to China, and much more. Her obituary in *The Times* in 1970 said: 'There is good reason to believe that no contemporary woman equalled or indeed approached her record of adventurous journeys in unfamiliar lands with modes of transport so varied and calling for determined and fearless achievement of her objectives. At various times she had pressed into service horses, mules, yak and reindeer in addition to cars and aircraft.'

Why did she do it? A major interest was archaeology but she also visited areas in political or military turmoil, such as Ethiopia and Eritrea in 1935, and interviewed political figures such as the Chinese leader, Mao Tse-Tung. She was a war correspondent for the *Daily Express* during the Second World War and at the Nuremberg trials. She had a keen intelligence and used it in her travels, so much so that it has been suggested she was working for the British Secret Service, at least part of the time.

Sadly Violet outlived all her children and her second husband, Francis Fisher, who died in 1956. Little Ocean and Forest are buried here at Langleybury, and her first son, William, was killed in the RAF in 1945 and is remembered on the nearby war memorial.

LEMSFORD

LORD MOUNT STEPHEN AND THE CANADIAN PACIFIC RAILWAY

The Canadian Pacific Railway is one of the engineering wonders of the world – an immense achievement that once in existence seems to have always been an inevitable necessity, but which might never have been completed without the energy, courage and commercial ability of the man who lies here in Lemsford churchyard, beneath an unassuming cross. There is nothing here to show that he was one of the creators of modern-day Canada.

Lord Mount Stephen's railed plot.

HERTFORDSHIRE Who Lies Beneath?

George Stephen was born in 1829 in north-east Scotland. With eight children, his family had little money and he recalled working all summer on a neighbour's croft to earn enough money to buy shoes to get him to school in the winter. When old enough he was apprenticed to a draper in Aberdeen but came to London, like so many before and since, to make something of himself. By a lucky chance, he was offered an opening with his uncle's drapery business in Montreal and, at the age of 21, Stephen was on his way to Canada and an enormously successful future.

In the 1870s Canada was still largely virgin territory and the railways had made little impression on its vast interior. The money – and nerve – needed to bankroll and build a railroad defeated many an entrepreneur. Stephen, who had done well with the Montreal business, made his first move into this territory in 1876 when he and a group of investors bought the bankrupt St Paul and Pacific Railroad Company. By the time the renamed St Paul, Minneapolis and Manitoba Railway had proved a commercial success, Stephen's status in the business community and his wealth were assured.

Three years later he and his partners became part of a syndicate that took over the building of the prospective Canadian Pacific Railway from the Canadian Government, which was beset with problems and was happy to hand over the responsibility – and a substantial grant of money and land. There were just another 2,000 miles of track to lay, across the vast untouched prairies and most daunting of all, over, or through, the great Rocky Mountains!

It took Stephen and his company just four years and the through service to Vancouver opened for business in the spring of 1886. He worked with great men, especially William Van Horne as general manager, but a great part of the company's success was down to George Stephen himself, who was a born leader and combined energy, nerve and diplomacy in his dealings – 'in his presence doubt and difficulties vanished and hope and confidence revived,' a friend said after his death. He also had a vision that extended beyond mere railway tracks. For him, the job would not be completed 'until one end rested in Liverpool and the other in Yokohama and Hong Kong', bringing the world closer together. It was one of the great romantic engineering enterprises of the Victorian era that thrilled newspaper readers of the day and can still strike awe into anyone who considers the practical difficulties he and his men faced.

One of the obstructions in the way, for instance, was Kicking Horse Pass, 5,339 ft high, on the Alberta/British Columbia border. Known to the men of the Canadian Pacific as the 'Big Hill', they reached it in 1884 and had to build a temporary line over 'Mount Stephen'. It needed a gradient of 4.5% (1 in 23) and was the steepest stretch of mainline railroad in North America, so tough that heavy dining and sleeping cars could not be pulled up by the engines, so new stopping places either side had to be developed. So many accidents took place that it eventually became necessary to dig tunnels to replace the high route over the Pass, a less expensive option! It was designated a National Historic Site in 1971.

For his services to the Canadian people (and therefore by implication to the British Empire), George Stephen was created a baronet in 1886 and raised to the peerage in 1891. He took the title Lord Mount Stephen after the high peak in the Rockies, conquered by his engineers, surveyors and navvies, and named by them after him. In 1905 he was made a GCVO (Grand Cross of the Royal Victorian Order).

He retired more or less from business after he had seen the Canadian Pacific through, and came to Brocket Hall here at Lemsford in 1892 to enjoy another 30 years of philanthropic work. He made huge donations to charity in England and Canada, in particular as founder of the Royal Victoria Hospital in Montreal and a substantial patron of the King Edward's Hospital Fund in London. The latter received roughly £½ million from him during his lifetime and in his will he left them the residue of his estate, estimated at another £¼ million.

After the news of Stephen's death at Brocket Hall on 29 November 1921, at the age of 92, flags were flown at half-mast all along the Canadian Pacific route. He had outlived most of his contemporaries but his memorial service at the Chapel Royal, St James's Palace, was attended by the great and the good. Here in Lemsford his burial service was quiet and very private as he had wished. His coffin was brought to the church on a Canadian 'buckboard' wagon, the only flowers being a wreath of scarlet carnations, while members of his staff on the Brocket estate acted as bearers. He had been well regarded in the village, where he had built the villagers a reading room and a nursing clinic, and he was known there and in the wider world as 'a kind man who believed in hard work, and loved to see the results of creative effort and the prosperity and happiness they brought to others'.

LILLEY

TOUCHED BY WAR

Sometimes when wandering in churchyards a name or a phrase will set you wondering about the lives of the people buried there. So it was with two headstones side by side in Lilley churchyard, one marked by a rosemary bush – rosemary for remembrance. Here lie two widows, Beatrice Daisy Kirk and Martha Clarke, and on their headstones appear also the names of their husbands - Pte Harold Kirk of the 2nd/6th Battalion Sherwood Foresters, killed in action 1917, aged 28; and Pte Herbert John Clarke of the 2nd Battalion Bedfordshire Regiment, killed in France 30 September 1915, at Vermelles, aged 39.

As with every village in the country, Lilley was touched by the tragedy of the First World War, and both these ladies lived on alone for another 50 years. There were so many women like them, and women too who lost their men before they had time to marry, or who never had the chance to find a likely spouse because of the decimation of a whole generation of young men.

A little detective work soon begins to fill in some of the background. The Commonwealth War Graves Commission (CWGC) Debt of Honour Register confirms the deaths of the two men who were their husbands and gives more information. Neither of them lies here in Lilley – if they did, it would more likely be beneath the familiar neat, white headstone of the CWGC, but in fact their bodies were never brought home from the Front.

Beatrice's husband, Harold Kirk (Private 240914), died of wounds on 30 April 1917 and his grave is at La Chapelette British and Indian Cemetery at Peronne, east of Amiens in France. Peronne, on the Somme, had been taken from the Germans on 18 March that year (perhaps when Harold Kirk was wounded) – it was lost to them again in March 1918 and

A rosemary bush grows on the Clarke grave.

regained in September, only two months before the Armistice. The fighting claimed over 570 casualties who lie in the cemetery there with Harold Kirk.

Herbert Clarke (Private 3/6884), Martha's husband, according to the GWGC, died on 27 September 1915 and not on 30th September as shown on his wife's headstone. He has no known grave. His name is inscribed on the Loos Memorial at the Pas de Calais – at 'Dud Corner' to be exact, where they found so many unexploded bombs after the war that no other name seemed appropriate. The Memorial lists the names of over 20,000 officers and men whose bodies were never found after the biggest offensive of the war to date in that September 1915; the severity of the fighting and the heaviness of the bombardment meaning that not only were men blown to pieces, but also that a long time passed before bodies could be safely recovered. The battle at Loos was also the first time that the British used poison gas, the Germans having used it five months previously.

On the Lilley headstone, Herbert Clarke is said to have died at Vermelles – a small village three miles south of Cuinchy that was recorded in Robert Graves' autobiographical *Goodbye to all that* as 'taken and retaken eight times last October' (i.e. 1914). Only three-quarters of a mile from the British front line, little was left standing. It all seems a long way from this peaceful little place and it must have been unimaginable to the families left behind.

Herbert Clarke was Hertfordshire born and bred – at Offley, to be precise. He married Martha in 1897 and by 1911, living here at Lilley, they had eight children, aged from 14 years down to 1 year and 7 months. What made this middle-aged farm labourer with so many dependants volunteer for the army?

If you wander out of the churchyard through the lychgate and turn to the left, you will find the village war memorial, where Herbert's name appears alongside the nine other men from Lilley who died in those years. Harold Kirk's name is not here, however, for he was not a native of the village – he was born in Mansfield in Nottinghamshire and was living at Bolsover in 1911, the son of a coal miner and a miner himself. He married Beatrice in 1915 in Luton, and she must have come to live in Lilley at some time later after his death. His name appears on the Bolsover and Hillstown War Memorial in Derbyshire.

Harold's army service papers have survived and we find that he was 5 ft 6 inches tall, a fit young man but who only weighed 138 lbs and had a chest measurement of 35¾ inches. He had enlisted on 21 October 1914, but spent the next two years as a Reserve. He was sent out to France on 26 March 1917, and survived only 34 days. Wounded in the thigh and abdomen, he died at No 55 Casualty Clearing Station at Peronne. And then army paperwork began for Beatrice – she was awarded a pension of 18s 9d a week for herself and their child.

Perhaps the most poignant piece of paper is the letter sent to Beatrice when his personal effects were returned to her, for which she had to sign. The list simply reads: 'Identity disc, 3 stamps, cigarettes, pipe, photographs, diary, false teeth, belt, wallet.'

LITTLE HADHAM

WILLIAM HARVEY – THRICE WITH CAPTAIN COOK

Close by the main door of the lovely isolated church of St Cecilia is the grave of Captain William Harvey. The inscription says (and the last part has now been eroded and is unreadable):

In Memory of
CAPTAIN WILLIAM HARVEY
late of the R.N.
Who accompanied that Illustrious
Navigator Captain James Cook
on his three voyages of
Discoveries, who died July 12th
1807 Aged 65 Years.
Frequently having observed in the course
of his travels the wonderful works of the
Almighty and the words of Job truly verified
'He stretcheth the North over the
empty place, and hangeth the
Earth upon nothing' Job 26.7

William Harvey was born in London in about 1742 and made his career in the Royal Navy after some years in the merchant fleet. He joined the *Endeavour*

Captain Harvey's grave by the door to St Cecilia's church.

in 1768, under the command of Captain James Cook, then a little known but experienced sailor. This first voyage was sent out by the Admiralty, the primary object being to take members of the Royal Society to Tahiti to observe the transit of Venus across the sun, which it was hoped would help in the calculations necessary to map the solar system.

By the time Midshipman William Harvey had returned, three years later, he had sailed round the world from east to west, observed the transit of Venus in Tahiti, circumnavigated and charted the coast of New Zealand, and charted the east coast of Australia, both the latter being completely new lands. The first landfall in Australia had been named by Cook 'Botany Bay', in reference to the richness of the specimen plants gathered there by naturalists Joseph Banks and Daniel Solander.

In those days sailors were paid off after each voyage, even those in the Navy, and had to find another berth on their own account. Harvey made a short voyage on a ship called the *Scorpion*, but was back in time to sign on for Cook's second voyage in 1771. This time the Royal Society had commissioned him to look for the 'Great Southern Continent', *Terra Australis*, that was thought to be in the southern hemisphere, at that time a completely uncharted void; even though Cook's findings had already proved it unlikely to exist. By now Cook was a famous man.

Another three-year voyage, and now Midshipman Harvey had sailed the world from west to east, made the first crossing of the Antarctic Circle, and could count himself one of the first men to sail round the world in both directions!

Only seven men accompanied Cook on all three of his voyages, and Harvey was one of them, this time as master's mate. In 1776 they left England once more, making a further exploration of the Pacific Ocean and looking for the legendary North West Passage through the Bering Strait. On 30 October 1777, while Harvey was on watch, in the South Seas at Huahine, a local man who had been arrested escaped. Harvey had to take responsibility and was disrated back to midshipman.

In 1778 Cook's ships were the first European vessels to visit the Hawaiian islands, and in 1779 they returned there. After a month they set sail again, but the foremast of the *Resolution* broke and they had to put back into Kealakekua Bay to make repairs. Now things went terribly wrong. Arguments broke out between the islanders and the crews, and a small boat was stolen. Cook attempted to take the King of Hawaii hostage till the boat was returned, but the islanders turned on him. As his party retreated back to the beach, Cook was struck down and then stabbed to death. Amongst those watching from on board ship was William Harvey.

The islanders took Cook's body away, but later returned some of his remains to the ships following an appeal. The *Resolution* and *Discovery* had then to make the voyage home, under the command of Captain Clerke. Harvey had been promoted to third lieutenant and sailed on the *Resolution*; Clerke wrote, 'I have often heard Capt Cook in private conversation declare his intentions of making Mr Harvey a Lieut.' Obviously his demotion would not have lasted long if Cook had lived.

In 1790 he married Martha Plumer in Portsea. She was a girl from Much Hadham and in 1797 they bought Halfway House near Little Hadham and settled here, far from the sea. Probably nothing in Harvey's life eclipsed the memory of that last voyage from his memory. He made other voyages, but never again touched the glory of being a trusted friend of one of the best known men in the world.

NORTHCHURCH

PETER, THE WILD BOY

Just opposite the main door of St Mary's, Northchurch, is a small headstone that bears the simple inscription:

> *Peter*
> *the Wild Boy*
> *1785*

There is also a brass tablet inside the church that relates a little of the strange story of Peter and, over the past two and a bit centuries, interest in one of the most famous feral children in the world has not waned.

Peter – he had no surname – came originally from Hamelin, in Hanover. When he was found wandering, practically naked and unable to speak, he was

Peter the Wild Boy's burial was paid for by the government.

taken to a hospital at Zell. He was then probably about twelve years old, perhaps a little older. His origins were never discovered, but it seemed likely he had been either lost in the forest as a young child, or abandoned by his parents and left to fend for himself.

When George I was at Hanover in November 1725 he heard some of the stories going the rounds about the strange boy found at Hamelin and sent for him. Curiosity about Peter had even resulted in reports in newspapers around the world – the Hanover correspondent of the *St James's Evening Post* reported on 14 December 1725 that: 'He was walking on his hands and feet, climbing up trees like a squirrel, and feeding upon grass and moss of trees.' Peter was strong and agile, hated wearing clothes, and preferred raw to cooked meat, as well as grass and moss. Children like Peter still occasionally come to light today, and still raise as much interest in their ability to survive against what seem insuperable odds in the wild.

George I brought Peter back to London with him in 1726. Queen Caroline took an interest in him and put him under the care of Dr Arbuthnot. Tutors were found for him but no amount of teaching could bring him to speak articulately and he remained a 'wild boy'. He undoubtedly suffered some mental disability, though how much that was the result of his isolated early life no one can say.

Eventually the Court began to tire of Peter and he was put into the care of Mrs Titchbourn, one of the Queen's bedchamber women. She was a friend of James Fenn and his wife, of Haxters (or Axters) End Farm and would bring Peter with her for a visit in the summer months. An agreement was come to that James Fenn would look after Peter on a permanent basis, for £35 a year to cover his keep. When James Fenn died 30 years later, Peter went to live with his brother Thomas Fenn at Broadway Farm, and it was there that he stayed until he died.

Peter did have a tendency to wander, once getting as far as Norwich where he was imprisoned as a 'sturdy beggar'. Luckily for him, his fame was such that he was returned to the Fenns at Northchurch. After that, they made for him a heavy leather collar with an inscription on the brass rim: 'Peter, the Wild Man from Hanover. Whoever will bring him to Mr Fenn at Berkhamsted, Hertfordshire, shall be paid for their trouble.'

Northchurch became a magnet for visitors, as Peter and his story still aroused curiosity, and his life in the parish is well documented. Thomas Bland, the headmaster of the school at Berkhamsted, knew him and wrote a long memoir in the parish register that included a physical description: 'Peter was well made, and of middle size. His countenance had not the appearance of an idiot, nor was there anything particular in his form except that two of the fingers of his left hand were united by a web up to the middle joint. He had a natural ear for music, and was so delighted with it, that if he heard any musical instrument play'd upon, he would immediately dance and caper about till he was almost quite exhausted with fatigue ... All those idle tales, which have been publish'd to the world about his climbing up trees like a squirrel, running upon all fours like a wild beast etc are entirely without foundation; for he was so exceedingly timid and gentle in his nature that he would suffer himself to be govern'd by a little child.'

He seems to have been extremely fond of the Fenns and those who looked after him. When one of them died, in Peter's old age, he simply pined away too, on 22 February 1785. His burial and headstone, and the brass memorial inside the church, were paid for by the Government.

Amongst the visitors who came to see Peter, much as they would an animal in a zoo, were philosophers and literary men whose interest related to whether 'man in a state of nature is a mere animal without the use of fire, raiment and even speech' (Lord Monboddo). 'Did Peter have a soul?', they wondered. This kind of thing, coming from 'men of some eminence in the literary world' with 'strange opinions and ill founded conjectures' made the Reverend Thomas Bland angry. Using the language of the time, he wrote with the authority of 'one who constantly resided above 30 years in his neighbourhood and had daily opportunities of seeing and observing him': 'Notwithstanding that the extraordinary and savage state in which Peter was first found greatly excited the attention and curiosity of the public, yet after all that has been said of him he was certainly nothing more than a common idiot without the appearance of one.'

As the brass tablet says, Peter led an 'inoffensive life' – perhaps for us the greatest interest in his story lies in the reactions he provoked amongst so many people in his own time.

ST ALBANS ABBEY

AN ARCHBISHOP AND A MARTYR

The great Abbey church is not only the Cathedral of St Albans but also the parish church of the Abbey parish, a small area that covers the streets around the heart of the city. Funeral services are still held in the Lady Chapel for parishioners, and ashes placed in the Garden of Remembrance. The gravestones on the north side of the church commemorate not only those associated with the cathedral, therefore, but also people of the town.

Robert Runcie

Close by the chancel wall is the simple stone that marks the resting place of St Albans' own archbishop – the Right Reverend Robert Runcie. Described in one obituary as 'tall and elegant, urbane and witty', he was said to have the gift of making everyone to whom he spoke feel special. He became Bishop of St Albans in 1970, ten years before being elected the 102nd Archbishop of Canterbury, and remained very popular in the city.

It was a turbulent time to be at the head of the Church of England, and Runcie had to keep his balance during many squalls, including those over the ordination of women, homosexuality in the Church, and political tussles over the nature and responsibilities of 'society' after Prime Minister Margaret Thatcher

Archbishop Runcie's grave in the lee of the abbey wall.

had declared there to be no such thing. He had a very public incumbency and had to endure quite vociferous attacks at times from the press, particularly after he called for reconciliation after the Falklands War in 1982.

The highlights of Runcie's time at Lambeth Palace included officiating at the marriage of Charles, Prince of Wales and Lady Diana Spencer in 1981 – a union he was not hopeful about from the beginning – and joining Pope John Paul III in prayer at Canterbury Cathedral in 1982, at the time a quite dramatic demonstration of goodwill from one Church to another and a triumph for Runcie.

The kidnapping of his 'special envoy' Terry Waite in the Lebanon was a dark time. Waite had established himself as an intermediary for the first time in 1981, when he had gone to Iran to negotiate the freedom of three missionaries held hostage. For the last three years of Runcie's work as Archbishop, the whole country shared his anguish over the seemingly interminable imprisonment and rejoiced when the outcome was eventually a happy one.

Hardworking and a perfectionist, easy in his manner and an enthusiastic Berkshire pig-keeper, he was also a brave man who during the Second World War, as a tank commander in the Scots Guards, was awarded the Military Cross after two exceptional actions. In the first he took out a German gun emplacement. In the second, as the citation described: 'One of his three tanks was knocked out by an anti-tank gun and set on fire. Runcie discovered that one of his men was trapped in the tank and went across open ground under enemy fire in order to pull out this remaining man who was unconscious. He succeeded in getting him out.' Both events took place under heavy fire and it wasn't lost on him later that he was the first Archbishop of Canterbury since Thomas à Becket to have been into battle. His personal experience no doubt underlined his words during the thanksgiving service following the end of the Falklands War when he gently pointed out that people on both sides of war suffer grievously.

After he retired at the beginning of 1991, he was created a life peer and became Baron Runcie of Cuddesdon, Oxfordshire. His ties with St Albans had always remained strong and he returned to live here, serving as Assistant Bishop. When he died in 2000 of cancer he was buried here at the cathedral:

Rt Rev and Rt Hon Robert Alexander Kennedy Runcie, Lord Runcie of Cuddesdon, priest, born October 2 1921; died July 11 2000.

George Tankerfield

Romeland, to the west of the Abbey at the foot of George Street, is a green and peaceful place to rest from the busy city streets. A few gravestones still rise from the carefully-tended turf and there are seats placed to contemplate the ancient Abbey Gateway and St Albans School. But as you sit awhile, note the boulder stone that commemorates George Tankerfield, and reflect that on 26 August 1555 a man was publicly burned to death here for his religious beliefs.

York-born and living in London, George Tankerfield was a cook in his late twenties. His story is told in *Foxe's Book of Martyres*, a catalogue of those Protestant martyrs who died at a time when the country was going through a religious backlash under Mary Tudor, who was striving to return her country to what she perceived as the True Faith under the Catholic Church.

Perhaps George was typical of many people of the time, who turned against the Catholic faith because of the cruelties being done in its name in this fruitless

The triangular-shaped stone that acts as a memorial to George Tankerfield.

catalogue of burnings. However, he began not only to doubt his faith but also to talk openly to others of his change of heart and, as Foxe puts it, 'he began to be smelled out among them' by the authorities. He was arrested at his home and taken to Newgate Prison, where he was undoubtedly tortured before being 'brought to his examination' before Bishop Bonner, who urged him unsuccessfully to recant his new beliefs before giving him up to be burned at the stake for heresy.

It was important for the authorities that the burnings took place in prominent places so that as many people as possible would be warned of the dangers of religious opposition. The importance of St Albans as a market town and administrative centre meant that it was a prime choice for the execution.

George was brought to the Cross Keys in St Albans by Edward Brocket, Esq, the High Sheriff of Hertfordshire, and an Under Sheriff named Pulter, from Hitchin. People flocked to the inn to see him and hear him speak, some to damn him as a heretic and some to offer silent support, while the pyre was built on Romeland in front of the Abbey church.

As the hour of his burning approached George ate a loaf of bread and drank a pint of Malmsey wine, representing, he said, the communion he could not be allowed to take. Then, so Foxe, says, he asked for a 'good fire' in his chamber, took off his shoes and hose and stretched his leg into the fire, jerking it quickly out of the flames as he felt the heat. Foxe describes an imaginary conversation between flesh and spirit, the one urging George to repent and live and the other telling him not to be afraid of a good death – surely a terrible dialogue endured by many human beings before and since.

The sheriffs, meanwhile, had disappeared off to a wedding dinner at 'a certain gentleman's house, not far from the town, whither also resorted knights and many gentlemen out of the country'. They did not come back until about two o'clock in the afternoon, and at last George's waiting was over. They brought him down to Romeland, where they allowed him to pray before he was tied to the stake and the faggots of wood were placed around him. A priest tried once again to get him to repent his views but George cried out to the crowd, 'Good people, do not believe him; good people, do not believe him.' Then the town's mayor ordered the wood set alight and George's body was burned to ashes, scattered to the winds over the streets of St Albans.

ST MICHAEL'S

JOHN STARKINS – IN THE COURSE OF DUTY

St Michael's may appear to the visitor to be simply a part of St Albans, but local people know it as 'the village of St Michael's' and it is a little community in itself, around the church and the bridge over the Ver at the bottom of Fishpool Street. The parish is large and stretches for some distance northwards from the city.

Just over the road from the church is the entrance to the Gorhambury estate, owned by the Grimston family, Earls of Verulam (whose family vault is in the churchyard), and many people come to St Michael's church to see the famous memorial to their ancestor Sir Francis Bacon, in the chancel. It is an impressive piece of sculpture: Bacon depicted sitting in a strikingly relaxed pose, one hand supporting his cheek, and looking as if he has just dozed off – or is thinking deeply. There is no record of where exactly Bacon is buried, but it is assumed that it is here in St Michael's church, as he desired.

Two workhouse masters lie side by side.

The churchyard has been closed to burials since 1886 and many of the old stones have gone, some of them incorporated into the paths. There are two stones marking the graves of masters at the St Albans Union Workhouse – Thomas Baker, who died at only 38 in 1871, and his predecessor Joshua Howes, aged 52, who was 'beloved by all who knew him'. Fortunate paupers in the workhouse, if he was as benevolent a master as he sounds!

John Starkins

The police have always cared for their own, especially when a member of the force is killed in the line of duty, and a gravestone in St Michael's churchyard shows that it has been the case since the police themselves were formed.

The Hertfordshire Constabulary was created in 1841, the first time that the county had had a professional 'rural police force', and it was not universally welcomed; not only by the criminal element, but also by those who resented it as an invasion of privacy. Many of the new constables were looked on by their neighbours as little more than spies.

However, the police force offered young men a new and different job, with possibilities for promotion and a lifelong career, and John Starkins was one of those who left labouring jobs to, hopefully, better themselves. Twenty-five years old, he was a native of St Albans and had lived with his family in a cottage on the Redbourn road before being stationed further north in the county, away from his 'home patch', at Stevenage. On 2 November 1857, when he had been in the police force for only a few weeks, his mutilated body was found in a pond. His throat had been cut with such savagery that his head was almost severed from his body, and he had lain in the water for several days.

It seems that PC Starkins 'had displayed so much activity and intelligence that he was frequently employed upon occasions where in ordinary cases the services of more experienced members of the force are engaged'. In this case, he was sent to investigate a series of petty thefts around Stevenage, with orders to search baskets etc carried by labourers going home at the end of a day's work.

On Friday 30 October, his inspector told him to look out particularly for a 35-year-old labourer called Jeremiah Carpenter, who was believed by a local farmer at Norton Green Farm to be stealing his corn and was thought of in the locality as a 'bad lot'. Carpenter had also been boasting in the neighbourhood that no policeman should ever search him. PC Starkins was not seen again until a constable, out looking on the Monday following, saw a foot and hand sticking out of the pond by a field called Cooper's Braches. There had clearly been a fierce struggle in the vicinity, and a pair of handcuffs lay nearby, open as if ready for use.

Suspicion immediately fell on Carpenter, who had arrived home from work that Friday evening lame and limping, with his working smock bloodied and dishevelled. A neighbour testified that he had helped Carpenter after an 'accident' with a pile of logs had supposedly crushed his leg – though the injuries he seemed to be suffering could equally have come from a desperate fight. Grains of wheat were found in his cottage that matched a particular kind used by the farmer who employed him.

The problem was that all the evidence against Carpenter was circumstantial. No one had seen him with PC Starkins and all the supposed incriminating circumstances could be explained away – the blood, he said, came from a pig he had been ringing at the farm, his lameness was due to his leg having been crushed in the woodpile when he got home, the wheat – well, he worked sowing the wheat in the fields so a few grains could have got into his clothes. Also a fellow labourer threw doubt on whether Carpenter could have been at Cooper's Braches at the right time.

It seemed likely as the trial went on that Carpenter would, as many people thought, get away with it, and that seems the likely reason for a dramatic claim by a fellow policeman that he had heard Carpenter admit his guilt to another prisoner as he was being transported in the police van to the prison. Unfortunately, no one could corroborate his tale.

Carpenter's counsel reminded the jury that if it convicted on this inconclusive evidence they would be returning a verdict, 'the effect of which must inevitably be to consign a living, breathing human being, now standing before them in the full vigour of manhood, to a felon's death on the scaffold'. Not surprisingly, the jury returned a verdict of not guilty, though 'not proven' would have been a better description of their feelings, as 'we think there was great suspicion against the prisoner'. Carpenter walked free.

Many years later the grandson of the local vicar wrote in his reminiscences that Carpenter's wife had confessed at an early stage to Canon Bloomfield that her husband had indeed done the murder and that she had helped him to hide the body in the pond. As his wife, should she stay silent, she asked? 'My grandfather's advice was, that being his wife she could remain silent.' Which she did. However, it seems that Carpenter was a reformed character from that time on, in gratitude to the Canon for saving his life, so perhaps good did come of it after all.

John Starkins was buried here a few days after his death, on 6 November, and the headstone erected by Hertfordshire Constabulary.

John Starkins' headstone was erected by the Hertfordshire Constabulary.

SHENLEY

Nicholas Hawksmoor – 'architectus'

One of England's greatest architects lies in the churchyard of St Botolph's church at Shenley. The church itself was made redundant in 1972 and became a private residence in 1981. The main part of the churchyard is still accessible, but those graves around the church, including that of Hawksmoor, are now on private land and not open to the public.

Nicholas Hawksmoor was born in about 1661 in Nottinghamshire, but came to London to work for Sir Christopher Wren in 1679. Wren employed him as his personal clerk, and Hawksmoor became his best known pupil, beginning architectural design on his own account in 1690. In Hertfordshire, an early project was that of Broadfield Hall, near Buntingford. Perhaps better known is his work at Castle Howard in Yorkshire, and Blenheim Palace in Oxfordshire.

The tomb of Nicholas Hawksmoor, now on private land.
(Courtesy of Peter Buttle)

In the meantime, he was still working with Wren, who designed the new naval hospital at Greenwich. Hawksmoor and Sir John Vanbrugh supervised the building and Hawksmoor carried on working there as deputy surveyor and clerk of works for some time. In 1711 he was involved in the surveying and building of some of Wren's 50 new London churches. Hawksmoor designed six of them, including St Mary Woolnoth, St Anne Limehouse, and St George in the East. By now he was a respected and influential architect in his own right, and in 1723 he succeeded Wren as surveyor to Westminster Abbey.

In about 1715–1719 he had bought the house known as Porters at Shenley, and he apparently came to stay in the country when he was suffering particularly bad bouts of gout. Eventually, in the 1930s, Porters became the main 'block' of Shenley hospital, but has now been returned to residential use.

Nicholas Hawksmoor died in 1736, at his Westminster house, of an illness so severe that he had been rumoured to have died before it actually happened. He said in his will that he wished to be buried 'in Shenley churchyard, or some other churchyard belonging to a country village', and his body was brought home to Porters for the last time. He was buried here on 3 April 1736. 'Widow Hawksmoor' died a year later.

The original tomb gradually sank below ground level and it was rediscovered in 1830 and replaced. Later the stone had to be recut yet again. It reads:

PMS [Piae Memoriae Sacrae]
L [Locatus]
Nicholas Hawksmoor [Arm]ʳ
ARCHITECTUS
Obijt vice fimo quinto die [Marttii]
Anno Domini 1736
Aetatis 75*

In 1936, on the 200th anniversary of his death, a service was held in the churchyard and wreaths were laid on his tomb by representatives of the Royal Institute of British Architects and the Dean and Chapter of St Paul's. It was fitting recognition for a man who created some of the best-known buildings in England.

---

*I am indebted to Peter Buttle for the transcript of the inscription, and the photograph – his website, www.st-botolphs.com, has more information about the now-inaccessible churchyard around St Botolph's.

TEWIN

Diamonds and Doubts

Alfred Beit

There were probably few in Victorian high society who could have matched the wealth of Alfred Beit, whose family vault is in Tewin churchyard. Born in Hamburg in 1853, he was trained in the Amsterdam diamond trade and then saw the opportunity to forge out on his own in South Africa, a magnet at the time for young men with extravagant dreams. He arrived at the Kimberley diamond mines in 1875 and quickly made his fortune as a property speculator and diamond merchant.

It was there that he met a Hertfordshire man – Cecil Rhodes from Bishops Stortford. Rhodes had his own imperialist dreams, which would culminate in the founding of Rhodesia (present-day Zimbabwe) and Alfred Beit became a

The powerful memorial to Alfred Beit.

close friend and supporter. His fortune became even larger in the 1880s when he moved into the goldfields of the Rand.

Now in his mid-thirties, he came to England, wealthy, influential and a partner in the firm of Wernher and Beit, his co-owner being Julius Wernher who purchased the Luton Hoo estate near Harpenden. Alfred himself settled at Tewin Water, a magnificent Regency house. You have to wonder if Beit and Wernher had listened to Cecil Rhodes reminiscing about the beautiful Hertfordshire countryside! Alfred took with enthusiasm to life at Tewin Water and his role as head of a large estate, where he fielded a strong cricket team made up from the house and garden staff. 'Can you play cricket?' was apparently the first question any job seeker was asked.

He was, however, still closely concerned with Rhodes and events in Africa, and made many enemies in this country by his support for the Jameson Raid in 1895. It was an idiotic foray into the Transvaal that Rhodes hoped would lead to the creation of a South African Republic but which led instead to a House of Commons enquiry that unequivocally criticised those involved.

At least he redistributed a considerable amount of his fortune in philanthropic donations, both in his lifetime and through his will after he died here at Tewin on 16 July 1906, with Oxford University and universities in Germany and Africa, Guy's Hospital and the National Gallery receiving large amounts and many other smaller gifts towards projects related to new technology and medical research. He was buried in the family vault, with a special train laid on from King's Cross to bring mourners from London. Tewin Water went to his younger brother Otto, who made the village his home till his death in 1930.

Lady Anne Grimston

Here in Tewin churchyard is one of the most famous tombs in Hertfordshire, that of Lady Anne Grimston who died in 1710, the second wife of Sir Samuel Grimston of the Gorhambury, St Albans family. Not famous because of whom she was, but rather because of what happened to the tomb after her death. It seems highly likely that this woman has been the unwitting object of Victorian 'spin' on an old legend.

In Victorian times, a visit to this tomb was high on the itinerary of many a visitor to the area and the reason for their interest was that two trees – an ash and a sycamore – could be seen growing up and through it, splitting the

Lady Anne Grimston's tomb.

masonry. Lady Anne, it was said, was an unbeliever in the Resurrection and denied that man's soul was immortal, and she had issued the challenge that if she was proved wrong after her death her grave would be split asunder.

Well, the trees have undeniably been there since the early 19th century. But the Hertfordshire historian W. Branch Johnson, writing in the *Welwyn Times*, 1957, pondered on the idea that the legend was in fact created by a curate at Tewin, the Reverend John Steel, in the 1840s. He had been shown, he said, a long poem of doggerel verse, dated 1842, that painted Lady Anne as a 'light' woman – 'her gruesome deathbed – her bequest of beer to the gravediggers,

The tree growing through the masonry of the tomb.

whereby they all got drunk and fought each other – her cold, uncharitable burial'. The initials at the end of the verses, though hard to read, could have been 'J.S.'.

Could it be, Branch Johnson surmised, that the curate had seized on the curious phenomenon of the trees to produce a moral tale that would convince people of the truth of the Christian message? If he did, and it does seem the most sensible solution, the Reverend succeeded beyond his wildest dreams in creating a legend that has now lasted nearly 170 years.

WARE

Physick and Chloroform

William Mead MD

In Memory of
WILLIAM MEAD M.D.
who departed this life
the 28th of October 1652
aged 148 Years
and 9 Months
3 Weeks and 4 days

In 2008 the Ware Society paid to have the inscription on Dr Mead's stone recut by a local stonemason, as it had weathered so much it was becoming unreadable. It can be found by the path into St Mary's churchyard from the High Street. The new stone does look a little battered, but that is because when it was being lowered into place it was broken into five pieces and had to be put back together again.

This is in any case not its original place or form – the grave used to be marked by a stone slab atop a raised red brick altar tomb to the east of the church's south porch – but interest in Mead's story has ensured it is going to intrigue us for years to come. For, despite the clarity of the information, no one knows for sure who William Mead was, or whether he did in fact live to such a great age.

The story begins with the parish burial register of 1652, which produces the information that '*George* Mead, Doctor of Physick' was buried at St Mary's on

Dr Mead's new stone by the path.

4 November 1652, having died at Tunbridge Wells on 28 October. Yet there is no reference to Dr Mead's age, and it seems curious to say the least that it would have passed unnoticed and unrecorded. It was quite common for vicars or their clerks to add little snippets of interesting information to the entries in their registers and here, a few lines are added as a note detailing a bequest in George Mead's will for 'the Poore of Ware', to be paid out by the Overseers 'upon the Feast day of St Thomas the Apostle' at the George Inn. Definitely George, then, and not William. So, who was William Mead, who died so coincidentally on the same day as Dr George? There is no answer.

The mud is further stirred by the fact that the inscription had been renewed several times since the 17th century; probably twice in the 18th century and definitely in 1851 by order of the churchwardens. Did a stonemason make a mistake, misreading the weathered and almost illegible lettering? It has been suggested that the age was originally '48 years' and that mischief resulted in a '1' being added, or that Dr Mead was in fact 118 years old and a genuine mistake led to reading the middle '1' as a '4'.

There is also the fact that when, in 1781, a correspondent wrote to the *Gentleman's Magazine* about the curious stone, he quoted the 'original' inscription, which 'could scarce be read', as including '... being of the Age of 148 Years and 9 Moneths' (no mention of weeks and days) and continuing with more lines which were almost obliterated, but which seemed to be about bequests.

David Perman, in *Hertfordshire 1731–1800 as recorded in the Gentleman's Magazine*, makes the comment that there was a 19th-century chemist in Ware High Street who sold 'Dr Mead's Patent Medicines' and suggests that perhaps 'the evidence of longevity was added by an earlier chemist with an eye to the sales of his medicines.' An example of canny advertising, then? But would the vicar of St Mary's, or the trustees of Dr Mead's bequests, have allowed such a blatant hoax to be perpetrated? Maybe one day a document will turn up that explains the mystery of Dr Mead and his amazing longevity!

Edward Chuck

Many of the stones at St Mary's have long been cleared away to the side of the churchyard, but in the extension plot of land across Church Road an eye-catching sarcophagus marks the grave of Edward Chuck Esq, 'an eminent maltster of this town and magistrate of the court of Hertford, who died from the effects of a severe accident November 2nd 1852 in his 70th year.' He lived at 87 High Street, and was a prominent local businessman, being also a banker, barge owner and farmer.

Edward Chuck was thrown from his chaise in High Oak Lane, when his pony shied as they met a larger cart coming towards them. The shafts of the chaise broke and Edward and his passenger were thrown forward onto the hard surface of the lane, Edward badly injuring his knee. In fact, his injuries were so severe that the local doctors sent for a London surgeon, a Mr Solly, to perform an amputation. What made this unusual, however, was that chloroform was used in the operation.

Edward Chuck's memorial stands in isolated splendour.

It had then only been six years since ether had been used by a surgeon, followed by experiments with chloroform by Sir James Simpson. For the first time it was possible for a pain-free surgical procedure to take place without the patient having to be conscious throughout. Previously, surgeons had had to be quick, working against the clock if their patient was to have any chance of getting through the trauma of an amputation or an organ removal, which allowed no time for finesse or careful examination. Many patients did not long survive, for if the operation did not kill them, post-operative infection often did.

Edward Chuck's operation would have been the talk of the town. Many people, in the medical profession and the general public, felt that anaesthesia was unnatural and wrong: it was seen not as a blessing but as a foolish means of stealing the patient's capacity for thought and reason. It would be another year, in 1853, before Queen Victoria allowed chloroform to be administered during the birth of her eighth child – a royal seal of approval that went some way to making anaesthetics acceptable, but an event that the medical journal *The Lancet* decided simply could not have happened!

Edward apparently went into the operation fully aware of what was to be done and prepared for it calmly. The operation itself was a success, but perhaps from undiscovered internal injuries, perhaps from infection, sadly he died two days later.

Edward Chuck's – and Ware's – prosperity was built on traffic to and from London on the River Lea Navigation; his malt was carried by barge to the Whitbread and Courage breweries. Many of the people of Ware had their employment on the water and connections with river and coastal traffic, and next to William Mead's stone is that of Joseph Nelson, 'steersman, who died April 28th 1834 aged 41 years'. His epitaph reads:

Bound on a voyage of full length
And dangers little known
A stranger to superior strength
Man vainly trusts his own
But oars alone will not prevail
To reach the distant coast
The breath of Heaven must swell the sail
Or all the toil is lost.

WATFORD

GEORGE EDWARD DONEY – A STATUS SYMBOL

The bicentenary in 2007 of the Act for the Abolition of the Slave Trade prompted a new interest in the lives of black people in Hertfordshire and much work was done through Hertfordshire Archives and Local Studies in their 'Hidden Histories' research to investigate their place in society. By combing through the archives, many surprising references were found to African and Caribbean people, and to links between some of Hertfordshire's wealthy families and slavery in the West Indies. In 1768, a slave was even sold in Hertford itself, with the Mayor authorising the sale of a boy called Howard, the property of James and Mary Baillie, to Alexander Bell.

It also became evident that there had been strong support within the county for the anti-slavery movement as it gained momentum in the early 1800s. The Act for the Abolition of Slavery was passed in 1833, with slavery totally abolished in British possessions by 1838. The county has a special place in the movement, as it was at Wadesmill that its leader Thomas Clarkson was inspired to begin the campaign – the monument raised to him stands beside the A10. There is an interesting article about the 'Hidden Histories: Hertfordshire, the slave trade and its abolition', by Jill Barber, in *Herts Past & Present*.

It was in the late 18th century that the legal status of black people in Britain began to change – until then they were, in effect, slaves, not free to order their own lives and liable to be bought and sold, but the growing hostility to slavery was making itself felt. In 1722 an important case had involved a man called John Somerset who went to court to stop his owner making him go back to the West Indies against his will. Lord Justice Mansfield ruled that it would be illegal to forcibly remove Somerset from England, a milestone in the fight against slavery. However, it was also a legal ruling that black servants like Somerset had no right to wages or to receive poor relief from the parish if they fell ill or destitute, so that in reality they could either stay in servitude, or starve.

It was fashionable at one time for wealthy families to have black servants, as a status symbol or a decoration. Sometimes they were depicted as accessories in paintings of their master or mistress, as much a part of the décor as a fine horse or valuable pet. There is, for instance, a painting by John Wootton in Watford

Museum of Cassiobury House and Park in the late 1740s; the Earl of Essex, along with his family and friends, is shown enjoying the Park, and among the staff standing by is one black servant.

At Cassiobury, at least, he would have been well treated and respected, becoming almost part of the family and receiving a good education. The Earls of Essex seem to have had several black servants over time, all known under the 'surname' of Donas or Doney, from the Latin for 'gift'. There are references in the baptismal parish registers, for instance, to 'Charles, a negro formerly called Donas' (1727), 'Othello, a negro formerly called Donas' (1730), and, on 12 August 1774, to 'George Edward Doney, a negro, servant to the Earl of Essex, aged about 16 as presumed.'

George Edward Doney seems to have been born in about 1758 in the Gambia, from where as a boy he was taken to West Virginia to be sold into slavery on the plantations. However, his destiny was not to be played out in the colonies, since in the mid-1760s he arrived in Watford in the service of the Earl of Essex and was to remain with the family at Cassiobury House until his death. He certainly took part in the life of the community, as he is listed in the Militia returns for Watford 1782–1786. When he was buried, he was referred to in the parish register as 'a widower', but no trace of whom he married, or when or where, has yet been discovered.

George Edward Doney died on 3 September 1809; his grave is in the churchyard of St Mary's church in Watford, near the Almshouses, and his headstone is now a Grade II listed monument. The *Gentleman's Magazine* printed an obituary for him in 1809: 'He discharged the duties of a faithful and honest servant, acquiring the friendship of those of his own station; whilst his respectful attention and demeanour conciliated the universal good opinion of all those who had opportunities of witnessing his services.'

The verse on the headstone confirms his status. His baptism at St Mary's may have been an important rite of passage, suggested to have been perhaps the 'Freeman's Charter' referred to:

Poor Edward blest the pirate
Bark which bore
His captive infancy from
Gambia's shore

To where in willing servitude
He won
Those blest rewards for
Every duty done
Kindness and praise the
Wages of the heart
None else to him could joy
Or pride impart
And gave him, born a Pagan
And a slave
A Freeman's Charter, and a Christian's grave.

George Edward Doney was by no means the only African who arrived in Hertfordshire in the 18th century. An interesting result of the renewed interest in African roots in the county has been that it is a reminder, as Jill Barber says, 'that many people in Hertfordshire today have an African ancestor dating back to the time of the slave trade.'

WIGGINTON

James Osborne – Hertfordshire's first VC

James Osborne, born into a labourer's family in Wigginton, was possibly the first Hertfordshire man to be awarded the Victoria Cross.

The Victoria Cross is probably our most famous medal, instituted personally by Queen Victoria after the Crimean War. At the time there were no awards for exceptional bravery (or, as Victoria insisted, 'For Valour') and it took no heed of rank – the only thing that mattered was a man's 'conspicuous bravery or devotion'. The medals were made from bronze that came from the guns captured from the Russians at Sebastopol, and were first presented in 1857, the year that James Osborne was born.

Aged 23, Osborne was in South Africa in 1881, a private in the 58th Foot (Northampton) and engaged in one of 'Victoria's little wars' that peppered the

19th century. This very short conflict, lasting only a few months, we now know as the First Boer War, or First South African War; it resolved nothing and the Second Boer War would follow in 1899. Relations between the Afrikaaner Boers and the British authorities in South Africa had been strained for some time and when, in 1877, the British government annexed the Transvaal it brought matters to a head. In 1880 the Boers proclaimed an independent republic, which the British were in no mind to accept – too much land and wealth was at stake.

The British soldiers in their highly-visible red jackets faced a new kind of enemy on the veldt of South Africa – men with a cause and with no conventional army, but skilled marksmen who could use every inch of natural cover to harry and ambush, moving quickly on horseback to attack and retreat. James Osborne was one of only 3,500 British troops suddenly pitched into a guerrilla war against thousands of seasoned settlers.

A week before Christmas 1880, the first inkling of what they faced came with the loss of 155 officers and men dead and wounded in one attack about 35 miles from Pretoria. Five weeks later the 58th Foot (Northampton) and 60th (King's Royal Rifles) suffered over 180 losses at Laing's Nek on the Natal border. James Osborne was therefore in the thick of the fighting.

On 22 February 1881 Osborne was with a small party of men from the 58th Foot engaged in a skirmish at Wesselstroom. In typical sleight of hand fashion, one group of Boer horsemen retreated, drawing the mounted infantry of the 58th onward, who then found another large group moving rapidly up on their rear. A Private Mayes had his horse shot from beneath him and was himself shot in the leg, so that he fell to the ground. Osborne, safely under cover, had seen Mayes fall and watched as his comrade struggled to get up, only to fall again.

Inside the Church Room at Wigginton there is a framed citation describing what happened next and I can do no better than quote from it:

'He appealed to a Volunteer to let him have his horse to lead to the assistance of his comrade, but without effect, the Volunteer urging no one could reach the wounded man under such fire. Osborne therefore rode straight from the cover he was under to the spot where he had seen Mayes fall, between two and three hundred yards in front of a line of two score Boers. Having come up to Mayes, he managed to drag him up behind him on his horse and, slinging Mayes' rifle over his shoulder, remarked that "the Boers should not get even that". Meanwhile the other men had kept an accurate and rapid fire on the Boers. Both the men and the horse escaped, although bullets were striking all round them, one hitting Osborne's rifle close to where he held it.'

Four days later the British suffered yet another defeat at Majuba Hill. Osborne may have been there too, as men from the 58th were included in the troops that struggled to the top of the hill, 2,500 ft high. They found themselves in possession of the Boer camp without a shot being fired, but were then picked off by Boers who came out of the night at them from below. Nearly 300 men were lost that day, killed, wounded or taken prisoner. Queen Victoria wrote, 'Dreadful news ... Another fearful defeat', in her diary when the news reached her. After that the government came to an agreement that recognised Boer independence under British 'suzerainty', but that would not last.

James Osborne, VC.

Returning home after his army service, James Osborne VC worked as a farm labourer on the Rothschild Estate for the rest of his life. Did he follow the later events of 1899 to 1902 in South Africa in the newspapers – someone else reading the reports to him, as he could neither read nor write – remembering the dust and blood so far from this very green and leafy corner of Hertfordshire? He had a stroke in 1913, when he was 56, and died aged 70 on 1 February 1928.

In 2005 Berkhamsted Royal British Legion began a fundraising campaign with the aim of replacing the headstone on his grave, which had become almost indecipherable. In June 2008 the new headstone was erected, with the assistance of 2nd Battalion The Northamptonshire Regiment, and enough money had been raised to set up a trust to maintain it in the future.

INDEX